Quick Tech

Readable, Repeatable

Stories and Activities

by

Peggi McNairn, Ph.D., CCC/SLP

and

Cindy Shioleno, M.Ed.

Quick Tech Readable, Repeatable Stories and Activities

Published by the Mayer-Johnson Co. by arrangement with the authors.

Artwork and illustrations by Peggi McNairn

First Printing January 1994
Second Printing October 1995

For information, please contact:
Mayer-Johnson Co.
P.O. Box 1579
Solana Beach, CA 92075-1579
U.S.A.
691 550-0084

ISBN # 1-884135-08-0

Dedicated to the memory of

Archie C. Johnston

Foreword

Color red plant.
Color blue plant.
Color white food is good,
And you, too.

14-year-old young man
with cerebral palsy

The first person I ever met who used an augmentative communication system dictated the above text to his teacher by eye-pointing to Blissymbols and words on an E-tran board. He wrote it to a schoolmate on Valentine's Day, a transcription of the familiar quatrain that begins "Roses are red..." It was viewed by his teachers as creative writing. And in many senses it was.

It was creative in the sense that no one had told the young man what to write. It was creative in that it was not a fill-in-the-blank activity, like the vast majority of this fellow's instruction at that time. It was creative in that this young man used the resources at his disposal (i.e., his knowledge of the world, our spelling system, and an available symbol set) to communicate an idea to someone he cared about.

It was not creative in the sense that it was almost a word-for-word (or, symbol-for-word) transcription or copy of a preexisting and well-worn poem. Given wider symbol access or greater spelling accuracy, the transcription might have been even more exact. But given wider symbol access, more frequent exposure to texts, and opportunities to discuss them to communicate personal messages to others about a wide variety of topics, it might have been even more creative.

With the foundational experiences now offered in *Quick Tech Readable, Repeatable Stories and Activities* by Peggi McNairn and Cindy Shioleno, this fellow might have had greater access to his own thoughts and the tools needed to express them in writing. This book represents a nice starting place for educators and parents of young, school-age children with severe speech impairments, who would like to provide the means and opportunities for their children to interact with others during storybook reading.

My colleague, David Yoder, likes to distinguish between the activities of reading **to** and reading **with** children. Too often, children with disabilities are read **to**. An adult picks a story thought to be of interest to the child, reads it aloud, and seldom interacts with the child about the story during the reading. Interaction, if at all, takes the form of questioning about story details or rhetorical questions such as, "That was a nice story, wasn't it?" The causes of such patterns may be traced to past experience (e.g., that's the way my teachers read **to** me), cultural expectations (e.g., kids with disabilities can't interact like other kids), or other sources.

The authors of this text have gathered the materials and tools to enable educators and parents to begin to read **with** their young, school-age children. Strategies, stories, symbols, and other resources have been provided herein to help beginners (both readers and listeners) feel comfortable with reading experiences.

Readers should view this text as a resource in itself--a treasured resource, as you know if you have gone in search of accessible reading materials for children with severe speech impairments. It is not an all-inclusive collection of stories, strategies, or resources. It is a sizable collection of materials and ideas. *Enjoy and learn with your child.*

David A. Koppenhaver, Ph.D.
Director
Center for Literacy and Disability Studies
University of North Carolina-Chapel Hill

Table of Contents

Focus: Self-esteem and cooperative relationships

Introduction

Reading aloud to children as they grow and develop is a valuable activity that improves speaking, listening, reading, and writing skills. Research reveals that children who are read to are better readers and develop a lifelong love of reading (Durkin, 1966). Koppenhaver, Evans, and Yoder (1991) found that literate adults with severe speech and physical disabilities had been read to regularly by others (71% of the 22 respondents) and had observed other family members reading for pleasure two or three times per week (86% of the 22 respondents).

Reading aloud should be an integral part of the daily curriculum for all students. Through the reading aloud experience, Durkin found that children learn about the actual process of reading. For example, students learn that print is read from left to right, books have a top and a bottom, a beginning and an end, and that print has meaning. During the actual reading of the story and the follow-up discussion and activities, children hear many words. Many of these words will become integrated into their listening and speaking vocabularies and later into their reading and writing vocabularies.

About the Book...

This book is developed around ten stories written about everyday life experiences of most children. It is divided into four sections. The first section, **The Value of Reading**, gives a brief overview of the theories of literacy development. It also describes seven light-tech devices that can be used to facilitate the development of literacy skills.

The second section, **Instructional Strategies for Literacy**, describes three main components of many good literacy programs. Guidelines for implementing these strategies and suggestions for choosing books are also included.

The third section, **Readable, Repeatable Stories**, provides ten predictable stories. The stories have been adapted to include Mayer-Johnson picture symbols for communication displays for the nonverbal/low-verbal student. The stories were field-tested in several classrooms. They were found to be equally effective in developing literacy skills for students in both mainstream and special education classrooms.

The fourth section, **Final Notes and Tips**, contains a miscellaneous collection of information and resources. Informal assessment strategies, including portfolio assessments and literacy skills checklists, are discussed. Also, an extensive list of additional skill specific literature is provided.

Part One

The Value
of Reading

The Value of Reading

Different authors have hypothesized various theories regarding the development of language and literacy skills (Wilkinson, 1971; Durkin, 1970; Merritt, 1974). According to Merritt, the desire to communicate is the result of "strong, intrinsically motivated purposeful activity" (Merritt, 1974, p. 132). A child acquires language through constant, meaningful interaction with his environment enabling him/her to obtain immediate and positive feedback and reinforcement. Based on this theory, then, language develops as a result of needs being met. These theorists advocate the supposition that reading is no less a communication process than oral language. They further hypothesized that oral language learning principles might also be applied to the learning of reading (Merritt, 1974). More specifically, then those techniques used to facilitate language development in physically and mentally challenged individuals could also be used to facilitate the development of literacy skills.

Many writers have described sequential, developmental reading programs. Grace Goodall (1964) developed a skills ladder that many teachers continue to use as a guide for teaching literacy skills (Figure 1). This particular approach assumes that basic skills are in place when children enter the primary grades. However, such an assumption cannot be made about all children, especially those with disabilities.

FIGURE 1. SKILLS LADDER by Grace Goodall in *Designs for Reading Programs*, Shelley Umans, 1964.

Step 13	Using the Encyclopedia and Other Reference Books
Step 12	Using the Dictionary
Step 11	Using Parts of a Book
Step 10	Following Directions
Step 9	Inferring Meanings
Step 8	Classifying and Organizing Facts
Step 7	Finding the Supporting Details
Step 6	Finding the Main Idea
Step 5	Vocabulary Building
Step 4	Using Contextual Clues
Step 3	Using Structural Analysis
Step 2	Using Phonetic Analysis
Step 1	Basic Sight Words

More recently, researchers have hypothesized that instead of developing sequentially, reading, writing, speaking, and listening skills develop concurrently (Koppenhaver, Colemen, Kalman, and Yoder, 1991). According to this emergent view of literacy, learning to read and write, like the development of speech and language, starts at birth, or perhaps even before birth (Koppenhaver, Coleman, Kalman, and Yoder, 1991, p. 42). This theoretical perspective is significant in its impact on how educators should view emerging literacy development as well as how to teach and reinforce those skills. Obviously, most children begin school with the ability to understand and use language. This metalinguistic ability is necessary if children are to develop mastery over the written word. The metalinguistic process can be defined as the abilities that allow children to "analyze and talk about language itself" (Menyuk, 1976). It can be argued then that "Because the act of reading requires readers to stand back from language (i.e., to analyze it as an object) the strong correlation between metalinguistic ability and reading level is. . . essentially a metalinguistic task" (Flood & Salus, 1982, p. 62).

Building upon this emergent literacy view, Dr. Laura Meyers (1984) has developed a reading model using computers as a language scaffold to help students to develop literacy skills in the whole language environment. Using computers with synthesized speech output, her model bypasses the need for oral language skills, allowing language delayed or disordered children the experience of using spoken and written language to convey meaningful messages. Based upon her model, this language scaffold can be removed as the child develops language and literacy skills.

These authors agree with Wilkinson's statement that "Learning to read is a matter of language." This learning involves an overlapping, interconnection of linguistic and literacy skills (Koppenhaver, et al., 1991). Given that children enter school with certain metalinguistic abilities, teachers can concentrate on the interconnection of these skills which can be viewed as a "Reading Tree". The metalinguistic abilities provide the foundation for the basic skills that serve as the "roots" that "feed into" and "support" later developing, higher level reading skills (Figure 2).

FIGURE 2. READING TREE

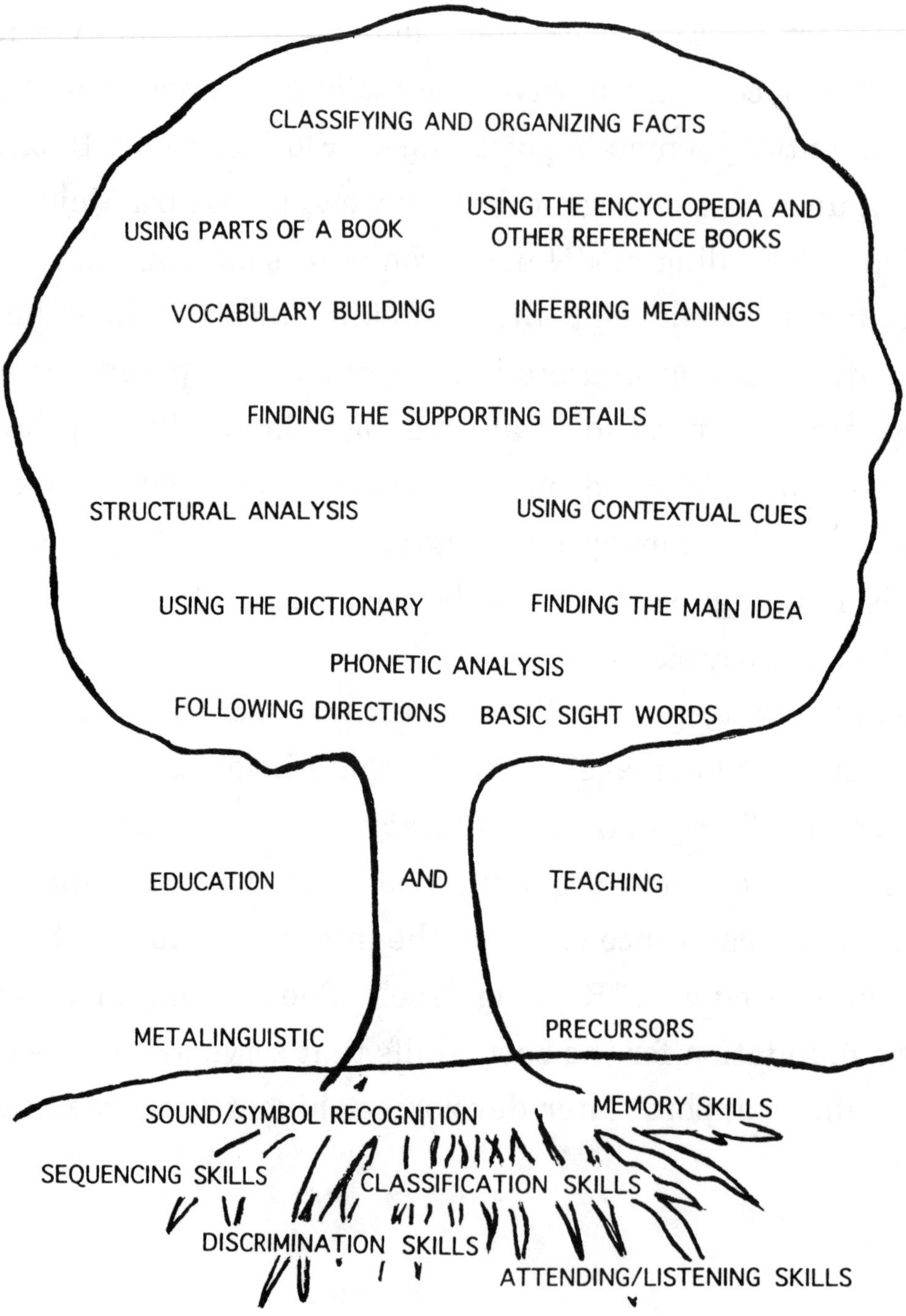

CLASSIFYING AND ORGANIZING FACTS

USING PARTS OF A BOOK   USING THE ENCYCLOPEDIA AND
                             OTHER REFERENCE BOOKS

VOCABULARY BUILDING   INFERRING MEANINGS

FINDING THE SUPPORTING DETAILS

STRUCTURAL ANALYSIS   USING CONTEXTUAL CUES

USING THE DICTIONARY   FINDING THE MAIN IDEA

PHONETIC ANALYSIS

FOLLOWING DIRECTIONS   BASIC SIGHT WORDS

EDUCATION   AND   TEACHING

METALINGUISTIC   PRECURSORS

SOUND/SYMBOL RECOGNITION   MEMORY SKILLS

SEQUENCING SKILLS   CLASSIFICATION SKILLS

DISCRIMINATION SKILLS

ATTENDING/LISTENING SKILLS

At the foundation of the tree are the metalinguistic abilities that children develop, giving them an awareness about language and its uses. It is the knowledge that language is an object that can be talked about, thought about, and manipulated that is essential before learning to read can take place, requiring the learner to shift attention from the meaning of language to the form of language. It includes skills such as segmentation (dividing ideas into words, and words into syllables and phonemes), phonemic analysis (breaking or analyzing words into phonemes or speech sounds), and blending (putting the sounds or phonemes together to form words) (Katims, 1993).

At the root of the "Reading Tree" are the basic skills necessary for the development of literacy and language. For example, these skills would include, but not be limited to:

- Attending/Listening Skills: The ability to listen and comprehend with thoughtful attention;
- Memory Skills: The ability to understand and remember information that has been seen, heard, or read;
- Classification Skills: The ability to group, sort, or categorize ideas or objects based on an established criteria, as when sorting blocks by size and color;
- Discrimination Skills: The ability to recognize or distinguish between two or more differing objects;
- Sequencing Skills: The ability to arrange information, ideas, objects, etc., in a specific order based on their relationships to each other;
- Sound/Symbol Recognition Skills: The ability to recognize and associate a written symbol with its corresponding sound.

These metalinguistic abilities and basic readiness skills then aid in the development of higher level, more sophisticated, reading skills. These higher-level reading abilities encompass such skills as described by Goodall's skills ladder. (See Figure 1.) (It should be noted that the skills listed on the Reading Tree are not intended to be an all-inclusive list of literacy skills.)

Although these skills are developmental, they are not always, nor should they be considered, sequential. However, it is the strategies used to present these very skills that create such a challenge to those who must teach those who are physically and cognitively involved. These unique students present a combination of various abilities and challenges. A comprehensive program must be developed to meet the specific needs of the individual students while, at the same time, allowing for the flexibility needed by creative teachers. It is the opinion of the authors that the existing research does not support any one method, program, or set of materials for meeting the educational requirements to teach all literacy skills.

Quick Tech Approach

To facilitate the development of literacy skills, a concise, easy-to-use approach, Quick Tech, was developed with specific techniques and devices that can be utilized at home and at school to deliver a systematic approach to teaching literacy skills. The goal of this approach to literacy and learning is to make access to technology in the classroom fast and effective, thereby reducing the amount of time spent on setting up learning activities.

Quick Tech is a process that expedites prompt access to technology which in turn increases communication and learning. This methodology encompasses the entire hierarchy of technology from simple, light tech devices to sophisticated, high-tech devices. The light tech end of the continuum is centered on the following simple adapted tools:

- The ReadIt Vest
- The ReadIt Window
- The ReadIt Frame
- The Rotary Dial Scan
- The Page-fluffer
- The Adapted Tape Recorder and Loop Tapes
- The ReadIt Sequencing Strip

The high-tech end of the continuum includes computers, adapted peripherals, and augmentative communication devices. In relation to literacy, the Quick Tech approach embraces the best practices of education regardless of their sources and does so through a functional communication-oriented method.

Quick Tech Tools

The ReadIt Vest

The **ReadIt Vest** is a vest that is worn by the reading facilitator at all times. Designed from Velcro-sensitive fabric, it provides one of the most versatile backgrounds for literacy development upon which objects, pictures, letters, or words can be displayed. With the physically challenged student properly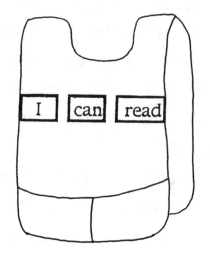
positioned, it becomes an ideal literacy tool for maintaining joint focus of interaction (McNairn & Shioleno, 1992 & 1993).

The ReadIt Window

The **ReadIt Window**, made of clear, light-weight lexan, provides another approach to eye gaze. It can be easily attached with Velcro to the ReadIt Frame or a computer monitor. The use of the ReadIt Window provides for ease in designing reading activities for the student with physical and visual limitations.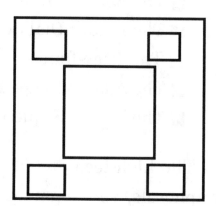

The ReadIt Frame

The **ReadIt Frame**, designed from CPVC pipe, is a frame upon which the ReadIt Window can be mounted for use on a table top or wheelchair lap tray. It resembles an upside down horseshoe with extending arms that allow its position to be varied.

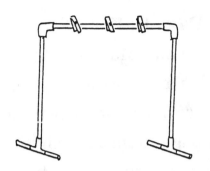

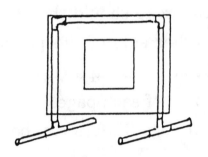

The **ReadIt Frame** can be used as a stand alone eye-gaze device when a ReadIt Window is not available.

The Rotary Dial Scan

The **Rotary Dial Scan**, a device that resembles a clock face, is a scanning aid that is switch-activated. Continuous pressure on a switch keeps the dial moving clockwise. Releasing the switch stops the dial. Long used as a communication device, it is equally effective as a literacy tool.

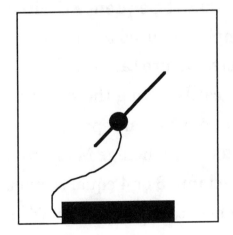

21

The Page-fluffer

The **Page-fluffer** (Cushing-McWilliams; Musselwhite, 1988) is a simple literacy tool that provides a space between each page so that the physically challenged student can turn the pages of a book. It is made by gluing a 1" square of tagboard

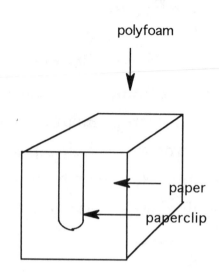

to a 1" square of sponge. One side of the paperclip should then be slid between the paper and the sponge. The other side of the paperclip should be seen on top of the tagboard. Attach the paperclip to each page of a book so that the sponge is on the back of each page. This will provide a space between each page. Several page-fluffers can be kept on hand for literacy activities.

The ReadIt Sequence Strip

The **ReadIt Sequence Strip** is a simple tool used to sequence objects, picture cards, and/or word cards, giving the student a concrete, visual representa-

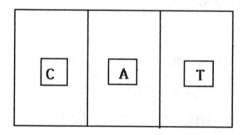

tion of sequencing. Made from clear, lightweight lexan, the strip is divided into 3 or 4 equal sections. Objects, pictures, or word cards can be attached to each section with Velcro to illustrate the sequence of a literacy concept. The ReadIt Sequence Strip can be attached to the ReadIt Frame or used alone, placed flat on the tabletop.

Adapted Tape Recorders and Loop Tapes

Adapted tape recorders are a very effective, inexpensive way to include children with disabilities in oral reading activities. Standard tape recorders can be adapted by inserting a switch directly into the remote microphone jack or by placing a battery adapter into the battery compartment and then attaching the switch to the adapter. Continuous pressure on the switch activates the tape recorder until the switch is released.

Loop tapes, when combined with adapted tape recorders, provide a powerful literacy tool for the student with disablities. Loop tapes are audiocassettes used in answering machines for outgoing messages that continuously repeat the message. The tapes are particularly useful when used with repeatable stories to introduce oral reading activities. The repetitive chant, line, or phrase can be recorded onto the loop tape. The nonverbal student can participate in oral reading activities by pressing a switch to activate the tape. (See Part 4, Readable, Repeatable Hierarchy.)

For more suggestions on the use of Quick Tech tools, see the *Ideas* section with each story.

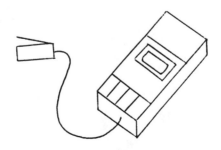

Part Two

Instructional Strategies for Literacy

Instructional Strategies for Literacy

Reading Aloud

According to the Commission on Reading (1985), the single most important activity for building the knowledge required for success in literacy development is reading aloud to students. Teachers at all grade levels should read aloud to their students every day. This should be a planned part of the daily language arts curriculum.

Guidelines for Reading Aloud:

■ Be confident and read aloud with enthusiasm and inflection.

■ Create a relaxed atmosphere of enjoyment.

■ Give a short oral introduction involving the students.

■ A discussion of the book should follow the reading. For younger readers, point to the pictures, make comments and ask questions. Older children can be encouraged to tell something they remember about the story.

■ Gather students around you informally to make sure all can see and hear the story. With a larger group, let them sit quietly at their desks and listen. Don't worry if they fidget. Let them draw quietly. It takes time to learn how to listen.

■ Show all pictures so no one will feel left out. Children should also be able to see the words in the book while you are reading.

■ Most of all, enjoy this special time each day.

Choice of Reading Material:

- Choose printed material with vivid characters and good dialogue.
- Be thoroughly familiar with the reading material; read it carefully before reading it aloud.
- Broaden students' basis of appreciation by reading a wide variety of printed material, including fiction, nonfiction, biographies, newspapers, magazines, etc.
- Read stories at a level beyond students' personal reading competency.
- Printed materials should suit the length of attention span of students.
- Add poetry and rhymes; after all, they were meant for the listeners' enjoyment.

The Shared Literacy Experience

Very closely related to the Read Aloud Program, the Shared Literacy Experience involves a teacher and a group of children sitting closely together while they share in the oral reading, rereading, and retelling of favorite poems, rhymes, and stories. Big Books are often used during this reading time. The Shared Literacy Experience is an excellent vehicle for introducing children to and engaging them in the act of reading. A teacher shares books with groups of children just as parents might share a favorite book with their children at bedtime. It is a more naturalistic method than many of the traditional approaches.

Guidelines for the Shared Literacy Experience Using Big Books:

- Seat the children as close to you as possible so that an "intimate" atmosphere is created. Make sure that all students can easily see the book. The use of an easel to prop up the Big Book will free the teacher for interactive reading.
- Briefly introduce the story. Point out the title, the author's name, the top and bottom of the book, etc.
- Read the entire story with enthusiasm. Subsequent readings will provide a vehicle for learning to read and the development of literacy skills. Rereading the book will provide opportunities for the students to recall vocabulary, ideas and information, refine nuances of language, and learn a variety of strategies and conventions including getting meaning from print and becoming familiar with the conventions of punctuation, spelling, and presentation.
- Talk about the illustrations, characters, or a favorite part of the book.
- Encourage the students to predict repeatable lines or outcomes.

During these readings, the teacher should aim to increase student participation, ultimately expecting the children to "read along."

■ Provide appropriate follow-up activities. These activities may include art, cooking, music, writing, and independent reading. It is important that small versions of the Big Book be available so that the children can read and reread their favorite stories.

The Choice of Reading Material:

■ Choose reading material with strong story lines and lots of action. Selections may include magazines, newspapers, novels, biographies, etc.

■ Read stories with characters and situations with which the children can strongly identify.

■ For younger students, some selections may be predictable, repetitious, and filled with rhythm and rhyme. Repetition and predictability allow the students to actively participate by joining in a chant or chorus that repeats itself frequently. Research indicates that this kind of repetition is important because words must be repeated many times before they are assimilated into a student's reading vocabulary (Rothlein & Meinbach, 1991).

■ Choose reading material filled with warmth, humor, and fun.

■ Select stories with attractive and appropriate illustrations that enhance the text (Rothlein & Meinback, 1991).

■ Ideally, the books would be available in two sizes: Big Books for group reading and small books for individual reading. (See Part 4, Big Books to Little Books.)

Uninterrupted Sustained Silent Reading

During Uninterrupted Sustained Silent Reading (USSR), everyone in the classroom, including the teacher, reads silently for a sustained period of time. Younger students may look at picture books. A free choice of reading materials is encouraged.

Guidelines for Uninterrupted Sustained Silent Reading

■ Provide a time for students to share books and magazines or newspaper articles.

■ Encourage the students to read aloud or tell about their reading experience following the USSR period.

■ Teachers should provide a brief overview or introduction to the reading materials available for USSR.

■ Each student makes several selections to read before USSR begins. No one is allowed to return books to the shelf or select more materials to read until USSR is over.

■ Begin with short periods of time at the same time each day. Twenty to thirty minutes is appropriate for upper elementary students. Shorter periods of time (five to ten minutes) are appropriate for beginning readers. For secondary students, individual flexibility is important as scheduling USSR may be more difficult.

■ Develop a comfortable reading area in which USSR may take place. Bean bag chairs, rugs, pillows, etc., set the stage for relaxed, enjoyable reading in the elementary school classrooms. For secondary students, a special, informal area can be developed in the school library to facilitate reading for pleasure.

Choice of Reading Material

■ Establish a class library/reading center. Provide a wide variety of reading materials reflecting the varied interests of students to meet a wide range of reading abilities. These may include student-authored books, newspapers, magazines, science fiction, autobiographies, etc.

■ Provide a selection of wordless picture books. This type of book develops independence and fosters a sense of reading (i.e., to learn to turn the page and to visually scan from left to right) particularly in children who may experience reading difficulties.

■ Students may want to bring their favorite books from home to share.

Part Three

Readable, Repeatable Stories

Readable, Repeatable Stories

The following section contains readable stories with repeatable lines. These stories have been adapted to include symbols from the Picture Communication Symbols manuals from the Mayer-Johnson Company. However, any symbol system can be used with these stories. Simply replace the existing symbols with the new symbols.

The format of the stories lends itself to the creation of big books for shared reading time as well as individual copies to be taken home. Each story is preceded with the following information:

- **Focus**: Literacy skill

- **Synopsis**: Summary of the story

- **Student Goal**: Suggested educational goal

- **Ideas**: Suggestions for expanding each activity

- **Literature Links:** Other stories with similar themes

At the conclusion of each story are the following:

- **Story Vocabulary**: List of vocabulary words contained in the story

- **Storyboard/Communication Display**: Picture/symbol display specific to each story

The repeatable stories are designed so that each vocabulary word in the story is represented on the storyboard/communication display. The symbols on each storyboard are arranged in a modified Fitzgerald Key format (McDonald and Schultz, 1973). For beginning readers or more physically challenged students, the teacher should highlight one to three specific symbols. By using color-coded symbols as cues, the students will be able to read the entire page by matching the color-coded symbols on the page to the color-coded symbols on the communication devices. For nonverbal students who are less physically challenged, specific vocabulary words can be programmed to each icon, allowing them to string words together to form the printed sentences. This method will also allow them to create novel utterances about the stories they are reading. The vocabulary lists can be sent home with copies of the stories and storyboards. It is important that these vocabulary words be taught in context so that they will be meaningful to the students.

We Like to Play

Focus
Positive self-esteem and cooperative relationships

Synopsis
This story describes many enjoyable childhood activities. The story emphasizes the fact that all children enjoy playing, especially with their friends.

Student Goal
The student will be able to apply the theme of the story to his own life.

Ideas

■ Have the children interview their parents about what they liked to play as children.

- Bring a favorite toy for show and tell.
- Cut out pictures of toys from magazines and catalogs. Using the rotary dial scan to sequence the symbols, use the pictures to create Rebus sentences.
- Record the phrase "I do too" onto a loop tape. When reading the story aloud, have the nonverbal students activate the switch to say the phrase at the appropriate time.

Literature Links

The Velveteen Rabbit by Margery Williams Bianco

Jessica by Kevin Henkes

Danny and the Merry-Go-Round by Nan Holcomb

Storytime, "Going to the Toy Store," by Pati King- DeBaun

Quick Tech Readable, Repeatable Stories and Activities, "Just Like Me," by Peggi McNairn & Cindy Shioleno.

My Friend Leslie: The Story of a Handicapped Child by Maxine B. Rosenberg

Hide and Seek by Al Shapiro

Ira Sleeps Over by Bernard Waber

We Like to Play

We	like		play	
		to		

My friends like to play cars.

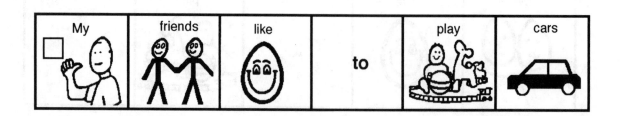

I do too!

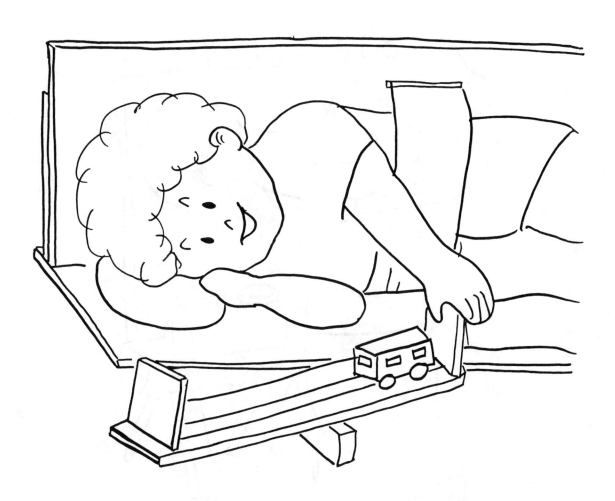

My friends like to play with paints.

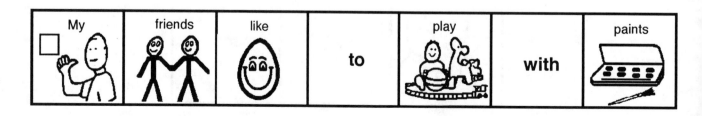

I do too!

My friends like to play fireman.

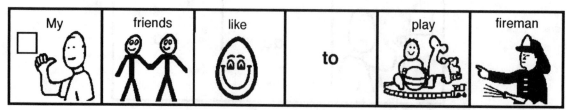

I do too!

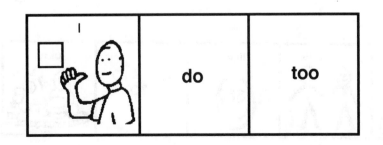

My friends like to play dolls.

I do too!

My friends like to play _____.

(Insert
picture
here)

I do too!

(Insert
student's
picture
here)

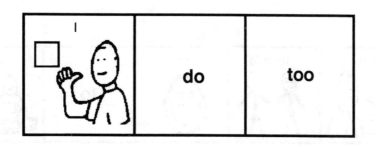

My friends like to play.

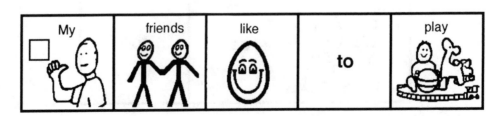

We like to play together.

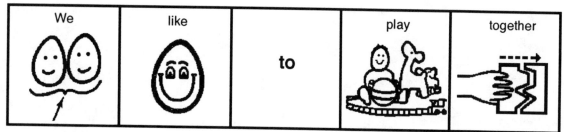

Story Vocabulary for
"We Like to Play"

cars	I	to
do	like	together
dolls	my	too
fireman	paints	we
friends	play	with

Storyboard for "We like to Play"

I	friends	car	like	
				with
My	fireman	together	play	
				to/too
We	dolls	paints	**do**	

In the Summertime

Focus

Compound Words

Synopsis

This story describes familiar activities that children experience during their summer vacation. The emphasis of the story is that all children like to have fun.

Student Goal

The student will locate and identify compound words in the story.

Ideas

- ■ Visit the community swimming pool and/or park. Be sure to take the necessary safety precautions.
- ■ Discuss summertime safety.

- Visit the local library during story hour.
- Look through magazines and cut out pictures of places to visit in the summertime.
- Display one half of a compound word on the ReadIt Window and ReadIt Frame and the other half on the teacher's ReadIt Vest. The student who is physically challenged can then eye gaze to match the two halves of the compound word.

Literature Links

It's Your Turn at Bat by Barbara Aiello and Jeffrey Shulman

Spot Goes to the Beach by Eric Hill

Rosie's Walk by Pat Hutchins

Picnic by Jan Omerod

Stringbean's Trip to the Shining Sea by Vera B. Williams

In the Summertime

In	the	summertime

In the summertime, my friends like to go swimming.

So do I!

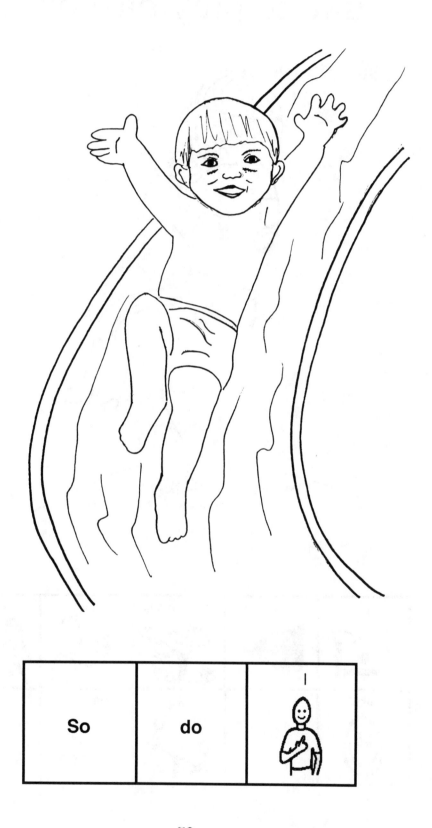

So	do	

In the summertime, my friends like to play baseball.

So do I!

So	do	

In the summertime, my friends like to go to the playground.

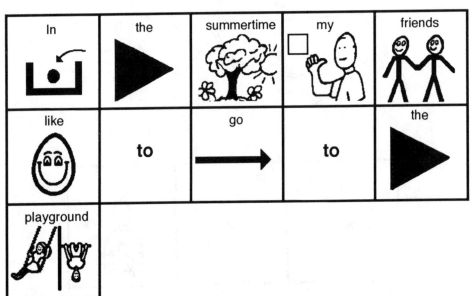

So do I!

So	do	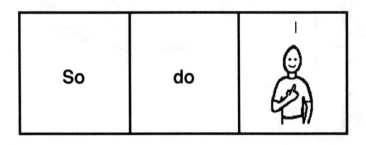

In the summertime, my friends like to checkout books to read.

In	the	summertime	my	friends
like	to	checkout	books	to
read				

So do I!

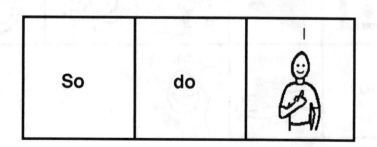

So	do	

In the summertime, we like to have fun!

Story Vocabulary for "In the Summertime"

baseball	have	read
books	I	so
checkout	in	summertime
do	like	swimming
friends	my	the
fun	play	to
go	playground	we

Storyboard for
"In the Summertime"

I	fun	checkout	play	in
my	playground	do	read	So
we, us	summertime	go	swimming	the
baseball	friends	have	like	to
books				

Just Like Me

Focus

Understanding the sequence of events in text.

Synopsis

This story relates the everyday life experiences of school age children. The emphasis is on the similar routines and activities that most children experience at school.

Student Goal

The student will retell the story in sequence using miniature objects, picture cards, and/or word cards.

Ideas

■ Sing the song "Wheels on the Bus." Use the "Wheels on the Bus" software from University of California at Los Angeles in the computer center.

- Visit the Principal's office.
- Ask the bus driver, janitor, cafeteria manager, and librarian to come speak to the class about their jobs.
- Talk about the importance of good manners in the cafeteria.
- Copy the pages of "Just Like Me." Using the rotary dial scan have the students sequence the pictures in the correct order. Remove the pictures from the rotary dial scan and place on the ReadIt Sequencing Strip.
- Record the phrase "Just Like Me" onto a loop tape. Nonverbal students can activate the switch to say the phrase at the appropriate time.

Literature Links

Miss Nelson Is Missing by Harry Allard

Math for Smarty Pants by C. Burns

Manners Can Be Fun by Munro Leaf

Quick Tech Readable, Repeatable Stories & Activities, "We Like To Play," by Peggi McNairn & Cindy Shioleno

Quick Tech Readable, Repeatable Stories & Activities, "In The Summertime," by Peggi McNairn & Cindy Shioleno

ABC of Things by Helen Oxenbury

Numbers and Things by Helen Oxenbury

The Ultimate Alphabet by Mike Wilks

Just Like Me

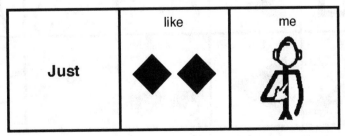

Just	like	me

In the morning, my friends ride the bus to school.

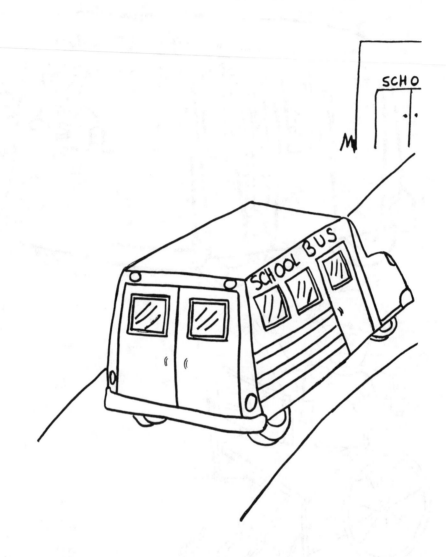

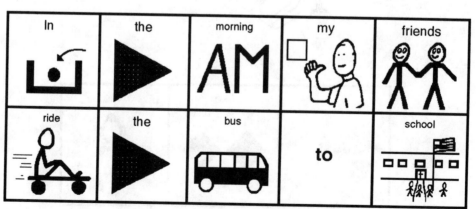

72

Just like me!

Just	like	me
	◆◆	

In class, my friends say the Pledge of Allegiance.

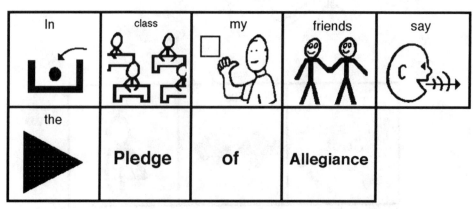

Just like me!

Just	like 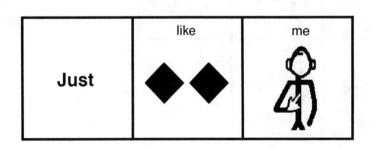	me

My friends have to read many books.

Just like me!

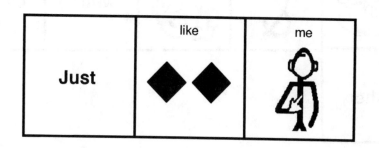

My friends look forward to lunch and talking with each other.

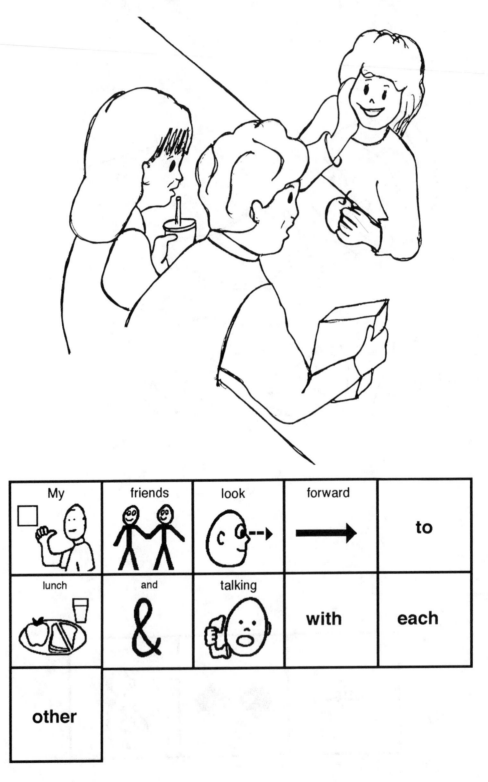

My	friends	look	forward	to
lunch	and	talking	with	each
other				

Just like me!

Just	like	me
	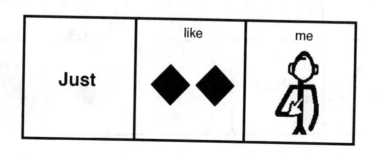	

After lunch, my friends work math problems on the computer.

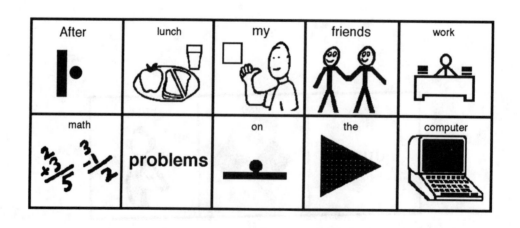

Just like me!

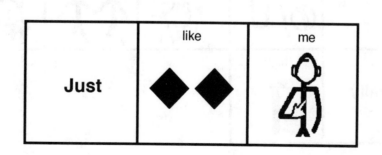

At recess, my friends swing really high.

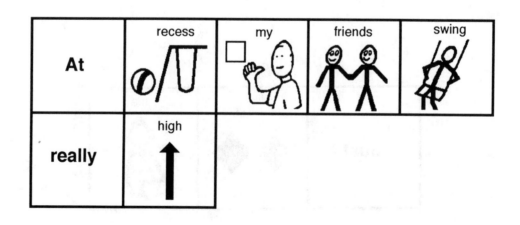

Just like me!

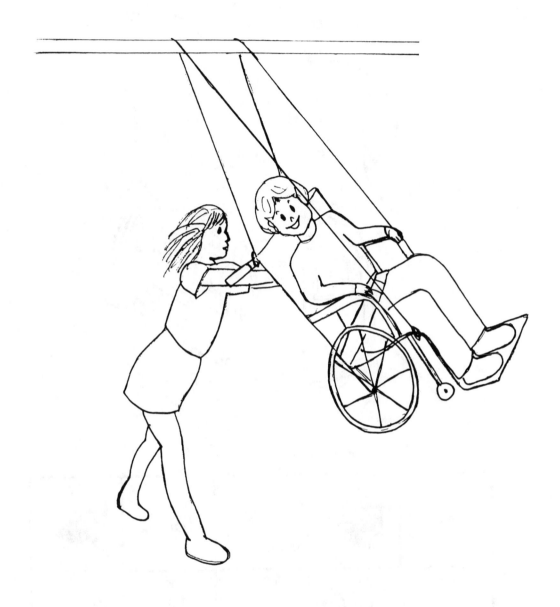

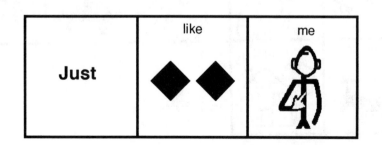

At the end of the day, my friends ride the bus home.

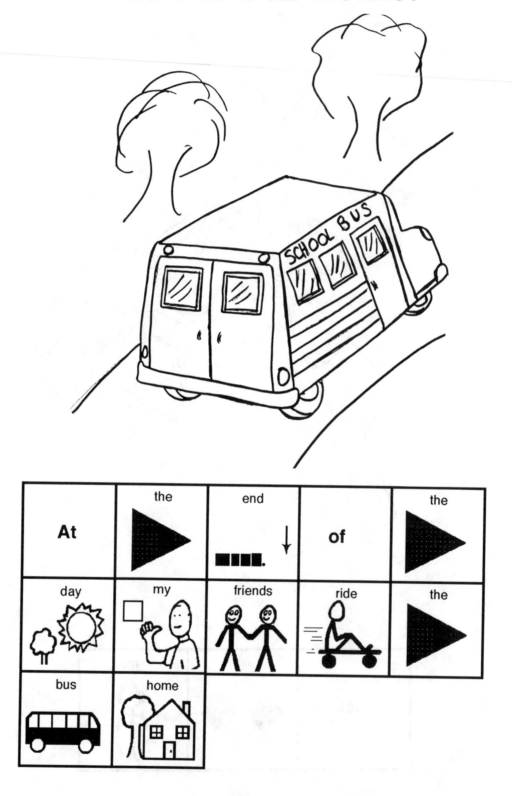

At	the ▶	end ⬛⬛⬛⬛. ↓	of	the ▶
day	my	friends	ride	the ▶
bus	home			

Just like me!

Just	like 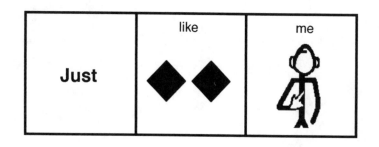	me

Story Vocabulary for "Just Like Me"

after

allegiance

and

at

books

bus

class

computer

day

each

end

forward

friends

have

high

home

in

just

like

look

lunch

many

math

me

morning

my

of

on

other

pledge

problems

read

really

recess

ride

say

school

swing

talking

the

to

with

work

Storyboard for "Just Like Me"

me	math	have	after	many
Allegiance	morning **AM**	like	and	my
books	**Pledge**	look	**At**	the
class	**problems**	read	**each**	on
computer	recess	ride	end	**other**
day	school	say	forward	**really**

Storyboard for
"Just Like Me" (cont.)

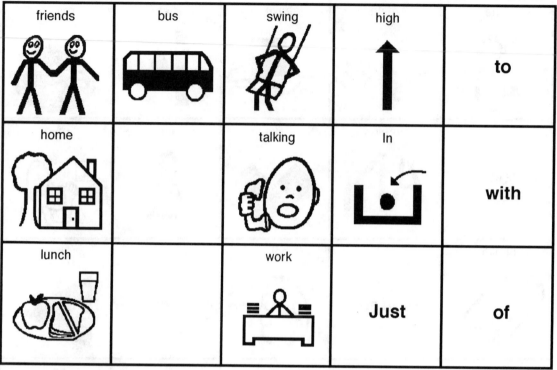

friends	bus	swing	high	to
home		talking	In	with
lunch		work	Just	of

At the Zoo

Focus

Predicting story events/ rhyming words

Synopsis

In this story about a trip to the zoo, the reader is asked to predict what animals he/she will see during his/her visit. The story is useful for relating real-life experiences to printed stories in the classroom.

Student Goal

The student will predict story events using real life experiences and contextual clues and patterns. The student will identify rhyming word pairs in the story.

Ideas

■ Estimate the size of any zoo animal. Mark its size on the

concrete/parking lot with a piece of chalk or masking tape. Measure each child's height to compare.

- Following a trip to the zoo, engage the students in a discussion to develop classification skills. For example, the teacher might ask which animals lived in trees, which animals lived in caves, etc. For nonverbal students, attach pictures of different animals to the rotary dial scan. They can scan to the animal in the correct category.

- Make a mural of zoo animals by gluing animal shapes to a poster board.

- Make rhyming word cards and attach to the rotary dial scan. Students can scan to the corresponding rhyming words.

Literature Links

The Carsick Zebra and Other Animal Riddles by David Adler

Great Gorilla Grins: An Abundance of Animal Alliterations by Beth Hilgartner

A Children's Zoo by Tana Hoban

Put Me In the Zoo by Robert Lopshire

Quick Tech Readable, Repeatable Stories and Activities, "I Want a Pet," by Peggi McNairn & Cindy Shioleno

If I Ran the Zoo by Dr. Seuss

Animal Fun by Peter Seymour

Busy Bears by Peter Seymour

At the Zoo

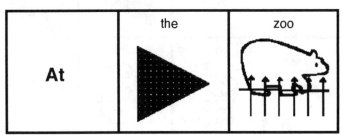

I'm going to the zoo today.
What do you think I'll see?

I'm	going		the	zoo	today
		to			
What		you	think		see
	do			I'll	

I'll see a kangaroo hopping to me.

I'll	see	a	kangaroo	hopping
to	me			

I'll see a lion growling as loud as can be.

I'll	see	a	lion	growling
as	loud	as	can	be

I'll see a giraffe looking through the trees.

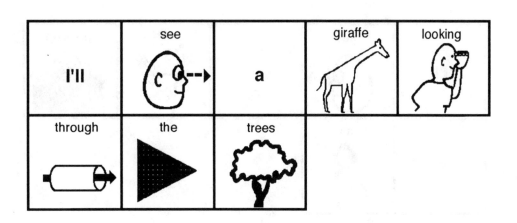

I'll see a deer peeking at me.

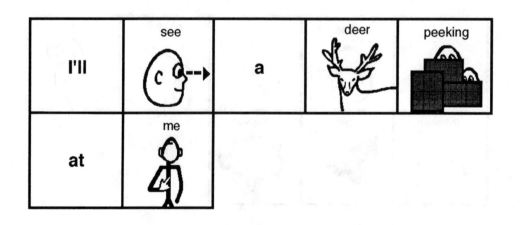

I'll see a monkey swinging from a tree.

I'll	see C -->	a	monkey	swinging
from	a	tree		

There will be a hippopotamus wallowing for all to see.

There X	will	be	a	hippo
wallowing	for	all	to	see

I'll see a tiger creeping up on me.

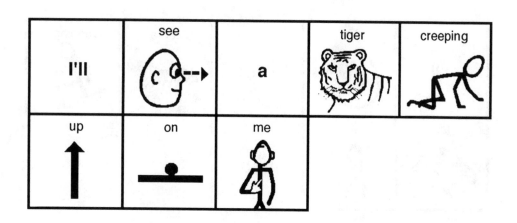

I'll see a zebra running fast and free.

I'll	see	a	zebra	running
fast	and	free		

I'll see an alligator hiding from me.

I'll	see	an	alligator	hiding
from	me			

I'll see a

(Insert
picture
here)

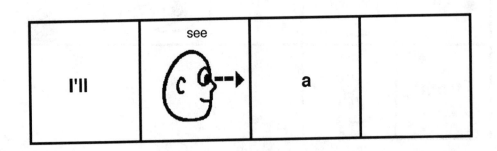

I'm going to the zoo today. There will be lots of animals to see.

I'm	going		the	zoo
		to	▶	
today		There		
		X	will	be
lots	of	animals	to	see

Story Vocabulary for "At the Zoo"

a	going	see
all	growling	swinging
alligator	hiding	the
an	hippopotamus	there
and	hopping	think
animals	I'll	through
as	I'm	tiger
at	kangaroo	to
be	lion	today
can	looking	tree
creeping	lot	trees
deer	loud	up
do	me	wallowing
fast	monkey	what
for	of	will
free	on	you
from	peeking	zebra
giraffe	running	zoo

Storyboard for "At the Zoo"

alligator	today	**be**	peeking	**for**
animals	tree/trees	**can**	running	**from**
deer	you	creeping	see	lots
giraffe	zebra	**do**	swinging	loud
hippo	zoo	fast	think	**of**
I'll		**free**	wallowing	on

Storyboard for
"At the Zoo" (cont.)

I'm		going		the
kangaroo	**will**	→	a	▶
				There
lion		**growling**	an	✗
		hiding	all	through
me				
		hopping	and	to
monkey			&	
		looking		up
tiger			as	↑
			at	What
				?

I Want a Pet

Focus

Short vowel sounds

Synopsis

The main character in this story wants a pet but has difficulty deciding on one. After listening to the kinds of pets each of his/her friends has, he/she finally decides what kind of pet he/she really wants.

Student Goal

The student will identify short vowel sounds in the context of the story.

Ideas

■ Visit a pet store.

- Cut animal pictures out of magazines and cut them in half. Attach to rotary dial scan. Let the students create silly critters by matching up different halves. Glue the halves together to make a collage.
- Invite a veternarian to talk to the class about responsible pet care.
- Record the phrase "I want one too!" on a loop tape. During shared reading, the nonverbal student can activate the loop tape to say the phrase at the appropriate time.

Literature Links

A Bug to Hug by Katherine Barry

Buddy's Shadow by Shirley Becker

I'll Teach My Dog 100 Words by Michael Frith

Quick Tech Readable, Repeatable Stories and Activities, "A Visit to the Zoo," by Peggi McNairn & Cindy Shioleno

The Cat in the Hat by Dr. Seuss

The Cat in the Hat Comes Back by Dr. Seuss

Who's Your Furry Friend? by Arnold Shapiro

The Digging-est Dog by Al Perkins

I Want a Pet

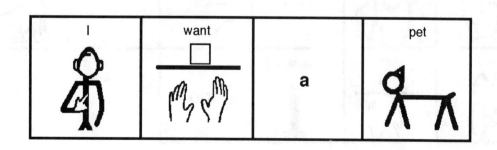

My friend Juan has a dog.
I want one too!

my	friend		has		dog
		Juan		a	

I	want	one	too
		1	

My friend Tamica has a cat.
I want one too!

My	friend	Tamica	has	a	cat
I	want	one **1**	too		

My friend Cindy has a rabbit.
I want one too!

My	friend	Cindy	has	a	rabbit

I	want	one 1	too		

My friend Tony has a bird
I want one too!

My	friend	Tony	has	a	bird
I	want	one **1**	too		

My friend Panha has a goldfish.
I want one too!

my	friend		has		goldfish
		Panha		a	
I	want	one	too		
		1			

My friend _____ has
a _____ .
I want one too!

(Insert
student's
picture
here)

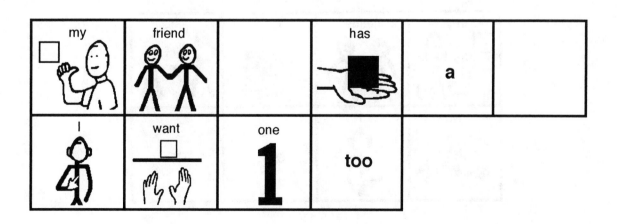

My friends have pets.
Now I do too!

my	friends	have	pets
Now	I	do	too

Story Vocabulary for
"I Want a Pet"

a	goldfish	Panha
bird	has	pet
cat	have	pets
Cindy	I	rabbit
do	Juan	Tamica
dog	my	Tony
friend	now	too
friends	one	want

Storyboard for
"I Want a Pet"

bird	rabbit		has/have	My
		Tamica		
cat	pet/pets		want	
		Tony		**a**
dog		I		one
	Cindy		**do**	**1**
friend/friends				Now
	Juan			
goldfish				
	Panha			**too**

I Can Do It!

Focus

Consonant blends

(This is also an excellent story for discussing positive self-esteem.)

Synopsis

The main character of this story is presented with everyday tasks that appear to be insurmountable challenges. The "can do" attitude helps the character achieve tasks that others often take for granted.

Student Goal

The student will identify consonant blends within the context of the story.

Ideas

■ Choose one child per week and have everyone in class tell or write positive comments about that child. Place the comments in a book to present to the student. This book can go home or be kept in the reading center.

- Create an "I Am Special" bulletin board spotlighting one child each week.

- Do a life-size outline of each student. Let the children fill in the details of the drawing. Hang the outlines on the wall around the room.

- Cut pictures out of magazines or take photographs of things that make the children happy or feel good.

- Attach consonant blend cards to the rotary dial scan. When the teacher reads a word aloud, the student will scan to the correct blend card for that word.

- Record the phrase "I can do it!" onto a loop tape. During shared reading, the student can activate the loop tape to read the phrase at the appropriate time.

Linking Literature

The Ugly Duckling by Hans Christian Anderson

The Smallest Boy in the Class by Jerrod Beim

Buster Gets Dressed by Rod Campbell

I Like Me! by Nancy Carlson

Howie Helps Himself by Joan Fassler

Patrick and Emma Lou by Nan Holcomb

The Snowy Day by Ezra Jack Keats

I Can Do It!

I	can	do	it

121

Mom says, "Wake up you sleepyhead."

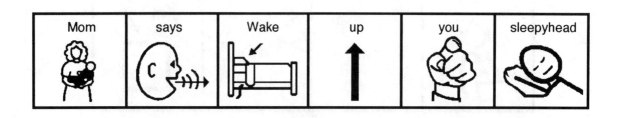

Mom	says	Wake	up	you	sleepyhead

"It's time to get dressed."
I can do it!

It's	time		get	dressed
□	(clock)	**to**	□	
I			it	
(person)	**can**	**do**	□	

Mom says, "Eat your breakfast."
I can do it.

Mom	says	eat	your	breakfast
I	can	do	it	

Mom says, "Brush your teeth!"
I can do it!

Mom	says	Brush	your	teeth
I	can	do	it	

Mom says, "Time to go! Buckle your seatbelt." I can do it!

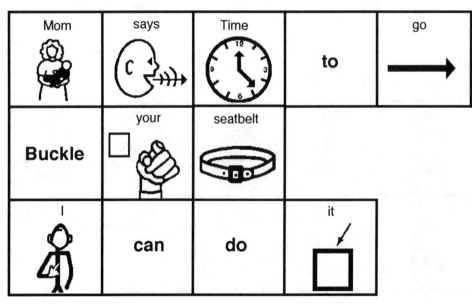

Mom	says	Time		go
			to	
Buckle	your	seatbelt		
I	can	do	it	

Mom says, "Put your lunch box away."
I can do it!

Mom	says	Put	your	lunch box	away
I	can	do	it		

Mom says, "Have fun at school!"
I can do it!

Mom	says	Have	fun		school
I	can	do	it		

Story Vocabulary for
"I Can Do It"

at	get	school
away	go	seatbelt
breakfast	have	sleepyhead
brush	I	teeth
buckle	it	time
can	it's	to
do	lunch box	up
dressed	mom	wake
eat	put	you
fun	says	your

Storyboard for
"I Can Do It"

breakfast	school	Brush	get	up
fun	seatbelt	**Buckle**	go	your
I	sleepyhead	**can**	Have	**at**
it/it's	teeth	**do**	Put	away
lunch box	Time	dressed	says	**to**
Mom	you	Eat	Wake	

Where's My Book?

Focus

Contractions

(This is also an excellent story for teaching spatial concepts.)

Synopsis

The main character in this story is in a hurry to get to school but has lost his/her book! Where can it be? The surprise ending will make the reader laugh.

Student Goal

The student will locate and identify contractions in the story.

Ideas

■ Involve the children in a library scavenger hunt. Have the students find books on different topics such as reference books, periodicals, newspapers, books by different authors, etc.

■ Develop a special reading center within the classroom to establish a print-rich environment. This center should contain a variety of books from the classics to student published works.

■ Encourage students to write stories about their interests. Publish these stories in a class anthology. This reinforces the importance placed on their reading and writing.

■ Establish a guest reading time. Invite a guest reader to read to the whole class (parents, grandparents, older students, etc.)

■ Print contractions and their corresponding words on cards. The teacher places a contraction card on her vest. Attach the corresponding word cards to the ReadIt Window. The physically challenged student can eye gaze to the appropriate word cards to match the contraction on the teacher's ReadIt Vest.

Literature Links

We Read: A to Z by Donald Crews

Over, Under, Through, and Other Spatial Concepts by Tana Hoban

I Unpacked My Grandmother's Trunk by Susan Ramsay Hoguet

What's Inside? The Alphabet Book by Satoshi Kitamura

Quick Tech Readable, Repeatable Stories and Activities, "I Forgot," by Peggi McNairn & Cindy Shioleno

Busy Bears by Peter Seymour

Hide and Seek by Arnold Shapiro

Where's My Book?

133

Time for school!
I've got to hurry!

Time 	for	school	
I've	got	to	hurry

Hurry, hurry!
Put on my jacket.

Hurry, hurry!
Put my book in my backpack.

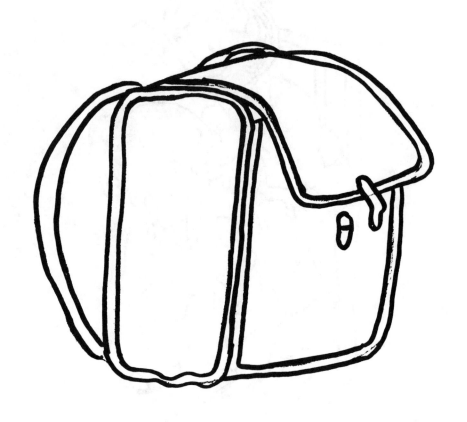

Uh-oh!
Where's my book?

Uh-oh		Where's	my	book

It's not under the bed!
Where's my book?

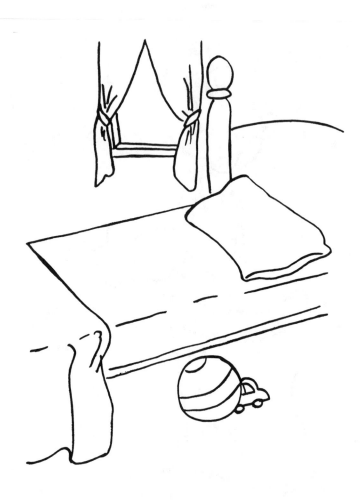

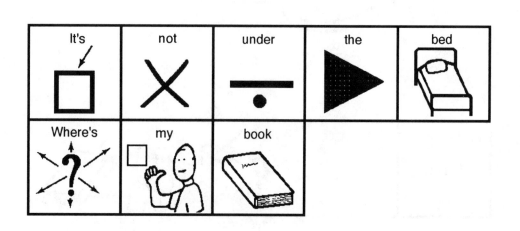

It's not in the closet!
Where's my book?

It's not on the table!
Where's my book?

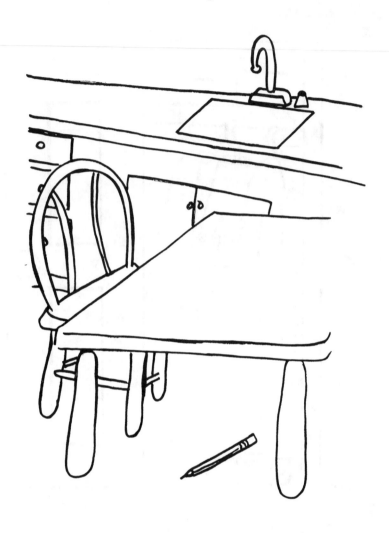

It's not behind the chair!
Where's my book?

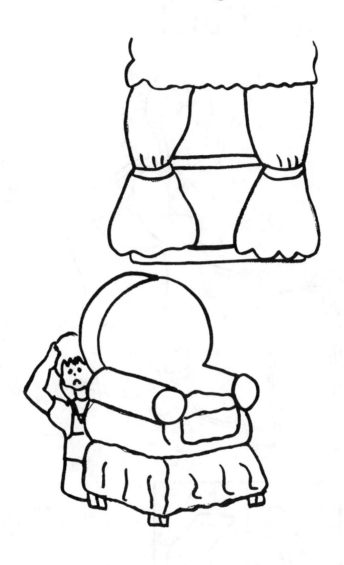

There's my book!
It was in my backpack all the time!

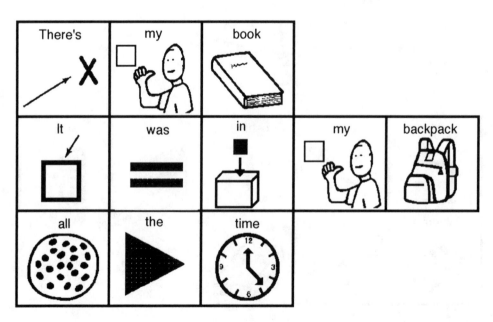

Story Vocabulary for "Where's My Book?"

all	in	table
backpack	it	the
bed	it's (it is)	there's (there is)
behind	I've (I have)	time
book	jacket	to
chair	my	uh-oh
closet	not	under
for	on	was
got	put	where's (where is)
hurry	school	

Storyboard for
"Where's My Book?"

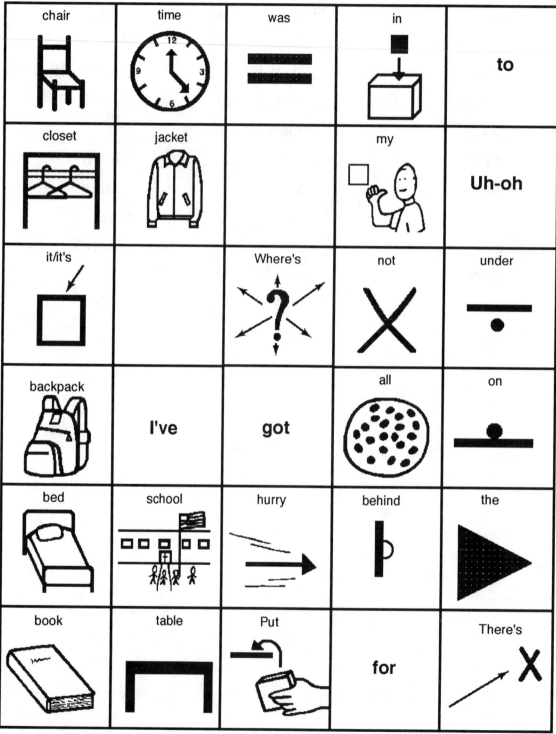

chair	time	was	in	to
closet	jacket		my	Uh-oh
it/it's		Where's	not	under
backpack	I've	got	all	on
bed	school	hurry	behind	the
book	table	Put	for	There's

When I Grow Up

Focus
Past-tense verbs

Synopsis
Deciding what to be when you grow up is often a very difficult decision. The main character in this story has the perfect solution.

Student Goal
The student will identify regular and irregular past-tense verb forms in the context of the story.

Ideas

■ Hold Career Day and invite guest speakers to tell about their careers.

■ Have students dress up as the occupation they would most like to have and tell about it.

■ Cut pictures out of magazines of different occupations to make a collage for the bulletin board.

■ Record the repeated phrase "I thought and thought and thought." onto a loop tape. During shared reading, the student can activate the loop tape to say the phrase aloud at the appropriate time.

Literature Links

Paddy Finds a Job by John Goodall

If I Ran the Zoo by Dr. Seuss

You Can Be Anything by Peter Seymour

Pippi Longstocking by Astrid Lindren Viking

If I Were in Charge of the World and Other Worries by Judith Voirst

When I Grow Up

When	I	grow	up

Today, Mrs. Brown asked us what we wanted to be when we grew up.

Today	Mrs. Brown	asked	us	what
we	wanted	to	be	when
we	grew	up		

I thought and thought and thought.

I	thought	and	thought	and	thought

Bill wanted to be a computer programmer.

Bill	wanted □ 〜 〜	to	be	a
computer 💻	programmer			

I thought and thought and thought.

Tasha wanted to be an author.

Tasha	wanted	to	be	a	author

I thought and thought and thought.

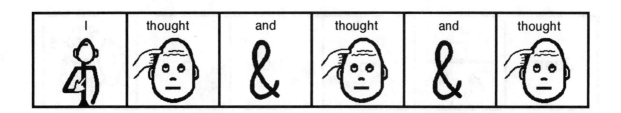

Juan wanted to be
a teacher.

Juan	wanted	to	be	a	teacher

I thought and thought and thought.

Su Ling wanted to be
a doctor.

Su Ling	wanted	to	be	a	doctor

I thought and thought and thought.

Vanna wanted to be
a rock star.

Vanna	wanted	to	be	a	rock star

I thought and thought and thought.

Suddenly, I knew what I wanted to be when I grew up!

Suddenly	I	knew	what	I
wanted	to	be	when	I
grew	up			

I want to be the best me I can be.

I	want	to	be	the
best	me	I	can	be

Story Vocabulary for "When I Grow Up"

a	grew	teacher
an	grow	thought
and	I	to
asked	Juan	today
author	knew	up
be	me	us
best	Mrs.	Vanna
Bill	programmer	want
Brown	rock star	wanted
can	Su Ling	we
computer	suddenly	what
doctor	Tasha	when

Storyboard for
"When I Grow Up"

author		we, us	want/wanted	
	programmer			**to**
Bill	rock star	**Juan**	asked	up
Mrs. Brown	**Su Ling**	**Vanna**	**be**	what
doctor	teacher	knew	and	
				a
I	Today	thought	best	Suddenly

Storyboard for
"When I Grow Up" (cont.)

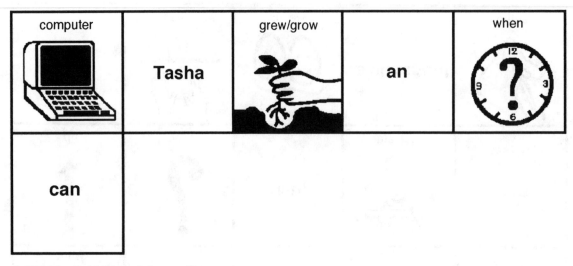

computer	Tasha	grew/grow	an	when
can				

I Forgot!

Focus
Punctuation

Synopsis
What seems like a really bad day full of forgetfulness turns out to be a good day after all.

Student Goal
The student will locate and identify punctuation marks including commas, periods, question marks, and exclamation marks.

Ideas

■ Tell personal experiences about forgetfulness.

■ Read sentences aloud to the class. Students hold up punctuation cards for ending each sentence. The physically challenged student can eye gaze to the punctuation card attached to the ReadIt Window and ReadIt Frame.

■ Look through other stories and find examples of each type of punctuation. Use the page-fluffer to turn the pages more easily for the physically challenged student.

Linking Literature

Don't Forget the Bacon by Pat Huchins

Alexander, Who Used to Be Rich Last Sunday by Judith Viorst

Alexander and the Terrible, Horrible, No Good, Very Bad Day by Judith Viorst

I Forgot!

I	forgot

Some days nothing goes right.

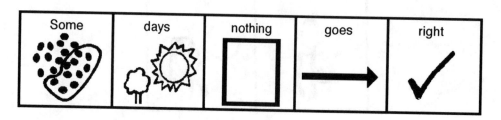

This morning Mom asked, "Did you remember to brush your teeth?" No, I forgot!

This	morning	Mom	asked	Did
↓ ■	AM		?	**Did**
you	remember	**to**	brush	your □
teeth		**No**	I	forgot

Grandma said, "Remember to make your bed."
I forgot!

Grandma	said	remember	make
your	bed		I	forgot

Later Sister asked, "Did you remember to pick up your toys?" No, I forgot.

Later	Sister	asked ?	Did	you
remember	to	pick	up	your
toys		No	I	forgot

Then Grandpa asked, "Did you remember to take out the trash?" No, I forgot.

Then	Grandpa	asked ?	Did	you
remember	to	take	out	the ▶
trash		No	I	forgot

After dinner, Grandma said, "Remember to put on your coat before you go outside." I forgot.

After	dinner	Grandma	said	remember	to
put	on	your	coat	before	you
go	outside		I	forgot	

At the park my friends asked, "Did you remember to bring the ball? I forgot.

At	▶ the	park	my	friends	asked ?
Did	you	remember	to	bring	▶ the
ball		I	forgot		

That night Dad said, "Remember to take your bath."
But I forgot.

That	night	Dad	said	Remember
to	take	your	bath	
But	I	forgot		

At bedtime, Mom and Dad said, "Remember to give us goodnight hugs." I didn't forget.

At	bedtime	Mom	and	Dad	said
Remember	to	give	us	goodnight	hugs
I	didn't	forgot			

Maybe it wasn't such a bad day after all.

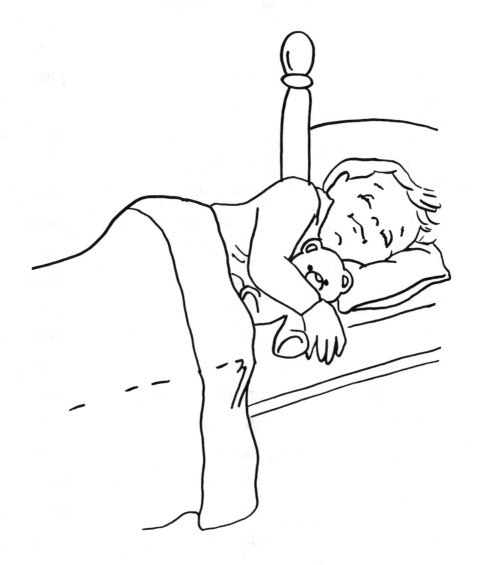

Maybe	it □	wasn't	such	a
bad	day	after	all	

Story Vocabulary for "I Forgot!"

a	forgot	park
after	friends	pick
all	give	put
and	go	remember
asked	goes	right
at	goodnight	said
bad	Grandma	sister
ball	Grandpa	some
bath	hugs	such
bed	I	take
bedtime	it	teeth
before	later	that
bring	make	the
brush	maybe	then
but	mom	this
coat	morning	to
Dad	my	toys
day	night	trash
days	no	up
did	nothing	us
didn't	on	wasn't
dinner	out	you
forget	outside	your

Storyboard for "I Forgot!"

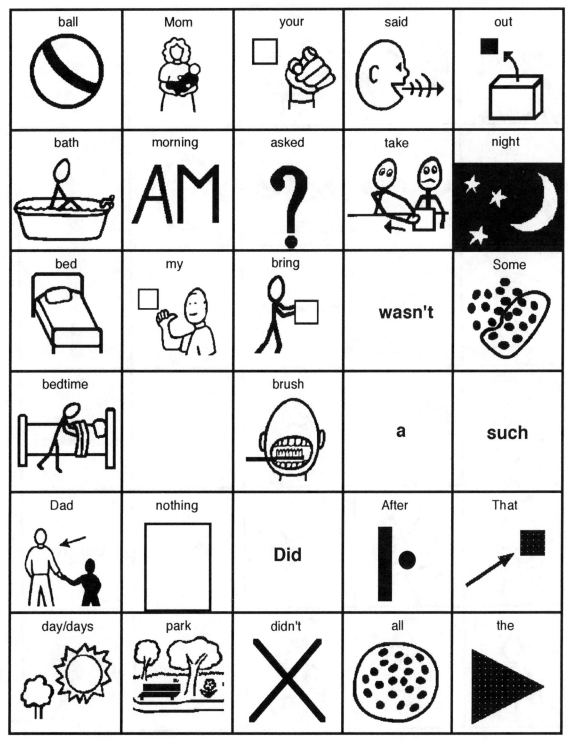

ball	Mom	your	said	out
bath	morning	asked	take	night
bed	my	bring	**wasn't**	Some
bedtime		brush	**a**	**such**
Dad	nothing	**Did**	After	That
day/days	park	didn't	all	the

Storyboard for
"I Forgot!" (cont.)

friends	Sister	forget/forgot	At	Then
dinner	teeth	give	bad	to
Grandma	toys	go/goes	But	up
Grandpa	trash	make	Later	on
hugs	us	pick	Maybe	before
I	you	remember	No	goodnight

But no!

Focus
Identifying the main idea

Synopsis
Little brothers and sisters can be such pests. The main character of this story suffers through a day with his/her little brother only to discover that he isn't so bad after all.

Student Goal
The student will identify the theme/main idea of a story.

Ideas

■ Bring family pictures to school and tell about younger brothers, sisters, cousins, etc.

■ Make a class graph of students and their siblings. Who has the oldest, the youngest, the tallest, the shortest, etc.?

■ Hold a little brother/sister/cousin day and invite them to eat lunch with the students in the cafeteria.

■ Record the phrase "But no!" onto a loop tape. During shared reading, the nonverbal student can activate the tape and read the phrase aloud at the appropriate time.

Linking Literature

A Smile From Andy by Nan Holcomb

Baby Sister Says No by Mercer Mayer

Quick Tech Readable Repeatable Stories and Activities, "We Like To Play" by Peggi McNairn and Cindy Shioleno

Butter Battle Book by Dr. Seuss

But no!

But	no

Some days my little brother can be such a pest!

Some	days	my	little	brother
can	be	such	a	pest

I try to play cars with him.

But no!

But	no

I try to read to him.

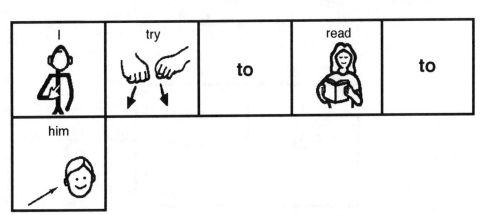

But no!

But	no

I try to play computer games with him.

But no!

But	no

There are days when my brother is a real pest.

There	are	days	when	my
brother	is	a	real	pest

I've thought about giving him away.

But no. I guess I'll let him stay.

But	no		guess	I'll
let	him	stay		

Story Vocabulary for "But no!"

a	giving	play
about	guess	read
are	him	real
away	I	some
be	I'll	stay
brother	I've	such
but	is	there
can	let	thought
cars	little	to
computer	my	try
days	no	when
games	pest	with

Storyboard for
"But no!"

brother	I've	are	thought	stay
cars	pest / be		try	a
computer		can		about
days	giving / to		no	away
games	is	when / real		But
him / let		with	Some	guess

Storyboard for
"But no!" (cont.)

I	play		such	little
I'll	read		There	my

Part Four

Final Notes
and Tips

Big Books to Little Books

Big Books are an integral part of the shared literacy experience. These oversized books contain text and illustrations that are large enough for the entire group of students to see easily. After hearing the Big Book read aloud one or more times, the students will be eager to read along as they become familiar with the story. Although there are many Big Books that are commercially available, teachers can make their own Big Books. Involving the students in this process will help to stimulate interest in reading and foster a sense of "authorship." It is strongly recommended that all of the stories in *Readable, Repeatable Stories and Activities* be introduced as Big Books. There are several different ways that Big Books can be made.

One way to make a Big Book is to select a favorite story and enlarge the illustrations using a duplicating machine or an opaque projector. The pages should be at least 25 inches by 15 inches. Once the text and illustrations have been enlarged, the students can color the illustrations in the Big Book. As a group, the students decide on the correct sequence for the pages. Once a logical sequence is created, the book can be bound. A heavy-duty stapler or metal rings can be used for the binding.

A second way to produce Big Books is similar to the above method except that the students are allowed to draw their own pictures to match the enlarged, printed text. The same procedure for sequencing and binding are followed. With student-made Big Books it is a good idea to create a book information page that lists the names of the illustrators and the date the book was made.

A third way to create Big Books is for students, either individually or in groups, to write and illustrate their own Big Books. The teacher should offer varying degrees of assistance, depending upon the abilities and needs of the students. Physically challenged students can be paired with "Reading Buddies" to create their Big Books.

A fourth method of making Big Books is with commercially available software. *Big Book Maker* from Toucan, *Super Print* from Scholastic and *BIG & little* from Sunburst are a few of the programs available for Apple and Macintosh computers. These computer-generated Big Books allow the teacher and students to create books that range in size from a six-inch card to a giant six-foot poster. The small version of the Big Books can be placed in the reading center/class libraries. The students may not know all of the words, but they can still enjoy "reading" the books all by themselves.

This is also a good time to encourage students to make books to take home and share. After selecting a favorite story that has been shared in class, duplicate the story for each student. Students can be encouraged to color the pages of the text, if appropriate. Each page of the story can be placed in a one-gallon plastic bag. Once all the pages are in bags, staple them together to form a "book." This is an inexpensive way to help protect the pages from moisture. At the end of the year, students will have a large collection of "Books in a Bag" to read over the summer with their family and friends.

Suggested Big Books for Shared Reading

The following Big Books are available from the Wright Group, 10949 Technology Place, San Diego, California 92127:

Grade Level - Kindergarten to First Grade

The Big Toe	*Lazy Mary*
Dan, The Flying Man	*Mrs. Wishy-Washy*

Grade Level - Kindergarten to First Grade

Grandpa, Grandpa

The Hungry Giant

In a Dark, Dark Woods

Obediah

One Cold Wet Night

Smarty Pants

Grade Level - First to Second Grade

Cat on the Roof

Clever Mr. Brown

Fast and Funny

Fiddle-Dee-Dee

Grandma's Stick

More! More! More!

Tiddalik

Wet Grass

Will I Never?

Yum and Yuck

The following Big Books can be obtained from Rigby Education, 4545 Virginia Street, Crystal Lake, Illinois 60014.

Grade Level - Prekindergarten to First Grade

The Enormous Watermelon

The Gingerbread Man

Jack and the Beanstalk

The Little Red Hen

A Monster Sandwich

Oh No!

The Three Billy Goats Gruff

The Three Little Pigs

The Ugly Duckling

Who's in the Shed?

Grade Level - First to Second Grade

The Bean Bag Mom Made

Breakfast in Bed

Debra's Dog

Excuses, Excuses

The Greedy Gray Octopus

The Horrible Black Bug

Munching Mark

Tricking Tracy

The Trolley Ride

When Lana Was Absent

Readable, Repeatable Hierarchy

Readable, repeatable stories, also known as predictable books, include repetitive language in the form of patterns, phrases, rhymes, and rhythms that help the reader to gain meaning from the text. Readable, repeatable stories encourage readers to actively participate by anticipating the repetitive chant or phrase and joining in the reading activity. This repetition is important because research shows that words need to be repeated many times before they become a part of a child's reading vocabulary (Reference).

When using readable, repeatable stories, it is important that the teacher be sensitive to the hierarchy of predictable books so that students will be truly successful.

Level 1 books have repeatable/predictable story lines or text that occur on at least every other page. The story itself has a predictable pattern. *Me, Too!* by Mercer Meyer and *We Like To Play* by McNairn & Shioleno are examples of Level 1 predictable books.

Level 2 predictable books begin to build in expectancy. Stories increase in length, with repeatable lines occurring frequently. *The Three Little Pigs, Three Billy Goats Gruff,* and *Are You My Mother?* are Level 2 books.

Level 3 storybooks have a predictable theme, but not a predictable structure or repeatable line. However, these stories do lend themselves to easy adaptation for repeatable story lines. Because of the structure of the story, the teacher can add his/her own repeatable line to encourage interaction. *Just Grandpa and Me* and *All By Myself*, both by Mercer Meyer, are good examples of Level 3 books.

Level 4 books are the highest level on the continuum of predictable books. These are stories in which the student can anticipate a similar structure, but the words and phrases vary. *At the Zoo* by McNairn & Shioleno is a Level 4 readable, repeatable story.

Each new level gradually builds upon the strengths and skills learned at the lower levels. By making sure that students are first introduced to Level 1 predictable books and are comfortable with the structure of predictable books, the teacher is setting the stage for the young reader to move successfully through the entire continuum of readable, repeatable stories.

Informal Strategies for Assessment

The goal of any assessment is to evaluate and record positive student outcomes based on observable teaching goals. Informal assessments should help students to understand the purpose of learning and to demonstrate their progress. It is an ongoing process that includes the teacher's observation of the students' interaction with written text as well as frequent samples of the students' work.

Portfolio Assessment

A portfolio assessment is a cumulative evaluation that documents and measures students' academic development of literacy skills by systematically building and assessing a collection of the students' best work. It provides holistic evidence of progress over a set period of time. Students are encouraged to collect their "best" work once or twice a week to add to their folders.

Portfolios can also build positive self-esteem, motivation, and responsibility for learning. A sense of pride will go along with "showing off" one's work collected throughout the year.

Literacy Skills Observation Checklists

A number of informal observation/inventories have been developed to measure knowledge of reading skills. These checklists can provide the observer with information about students' writing, reading, listening, and speaking skills. Also, by observing and collecting information continually, teachers send a message to students, parents, and administrators that learning is never completed; instead, it is an ongoing, evolving, growing, and changing process.

The following is an example of an informal inventory of literacy skills that has been adapted to the learner with special needs. Completing these checklists will give the classroom teacher an overview of the strengths and weaknesses of each of his/her students.

Literacy Skills Observation Checklists

_____
Student's Name

_____
Observer's Name

_____
Date of Birth

_____
First Observation Date

_____
Second Observation Date

_____
Third Observation Date

Mark: <u>Y</u> - Yes, skill is present   <u>N</u> - No, skill not present

<u>E</u> - Emerging skill

Complete the checklists for each of the four areas: reading, writing, listening, and speaking. The student should be given credit for responses that are written, oral, gestural (i.e., eye-pointing), or with assistive technology (i.e., communication device). When using the checklists over a period of time, the observer may use different colored ink to document the different observation dates.

Name_____ Date_____

Literacy Skill Observation Checklist
Reading

Sound Recognition
___Identifies common vowel and consonant sounds
___Can blend common vowel and consonant sounds

Word Meaning
___Recognizes familiar vocabulary words
(referential knowledge)
___Recognizes synonyms, antonyms, homonyms
(relational knowledge)
___Recognizes multiple-meaning words
___Uses context clues

Sentence Meaning and Structure
___Comprehends simple sentence structure
___Comprehends complex sentence structure

Reading Comprehension
___Identifies the main idea
___Locates and identifies details
___Distinguishes fiction from nonfiction
___Comprehends material from various sources

Memory
___Demonstrates directional concepts/vocabulary
___Sequence events of a story

Teacher/Therapist Comments/Observations:

Name_____ Date_____

Literacy Skills Observation Checklist
Listening

Attending/Listening
___Attends to oral directions/oral reading
___Attention is appropriate for age/grade level
___Responds within expected time limitations

Communication Skills
___Responds appropriately verbally or with assistive
   technology device to direct requests
     ___for information
     ___for clarification
     ___for action
     ___for attention
___Responds appropriately verbally or with assistive
   technology device to indirect requests
     ___for information
     ___for clarification
     ___for action
     ___for attention
___Provides appropriate nonverbal feedback
___Selects & maintains topic

Comprehension Skills
___Demonstrates understanding of verbal directions
     ___two-step commands
     ___three-step commands
     ___four-step commands
___Responds appropriately to oral questions
___Understands figurative language
     ___multiple meaning words
     ___sentences (metaphorical usage)
     ___slang (street language)
___Understands concepts of
     ___time (temporal relationships)
     ___space (spatial & directional relationships)
     ___quantity (quantitative relationships)

Teacher/Therapist Comments/Observations:

Name_____ Date_____

Literacy Skills Observation Checklist
Speaking

Language Structure-Sentence-Based System
___Uses sentences appropriately
___Asks questions appropriately
___Engages in turn taking (conversational)

Language Structure-Word-Based System
___Formulates grammatically correct sentence
    structure
___Uses a variety of sentence forms (questions, commands,
    statements, etc.)

Language Content
___Labels common objects correctly
___Uses age-appropriate vocabulary
___Uses humor appropriately

Pragmatic Considerations
___Understands conversation
    ___Makes comments/statements
    ___Requests information
    ___Requests action from others
    ___Requests clarification from others
    ___Requests attention from others
    ___Initiates and maintains topics appropriately
    ___Restates thoughts when requested
    ___Clarifies points when requested
___Relates information appropriately
    ___Clarifies when appropriate
    ___Sequences details of story

Teacher/Therapist Comments/Observations:

Name_____ Date_____

Literacy Skills Observation Checklist
Writing

Written Language Skills
___Identifies correct capitalization and punctuation
___Uses grammatically correct complete sentences in
    written work
___Uses a variety of sentence structures in written work
___Formulates written thoughts without frustration
___Using assistive technology writes a cohesive
    paragraph
___Sequences story topic
___Sticks to the topic
___Uses age-appropriate vocabulary
___Avoids fragments and run-on sentences
___Uses writing effectively to communicate information
        ___Sentences
        ___Paragraphs
        ___Reports
        ___Stories
        ___Letters

Teacher/Therapist Comments/Observations:

Skill Specific Literature

Letters/Sounds

Books Focusing on Awareness of Letters

Geisert, Arthur. *Pigs From A to Z.* Houghton Mifflin, 1986.

Hoguet, Susan Ramsay. *I Unpacked My Grandmother's Trunk.* Dutton, 1983.

Kitamura, Satoshi. *What's Inside? The Alphabet Book.* Farrar, 1985.

MacDonald, Suse. *Alphabetics.* Bradbury, 1986.

Schmiderer, Dorothy. *The Alphabeast Book. An Abecedarium.* Holt, 1971.

Weil, Lisl. *Owl and Other Scrambles.* Dutton, 1980.

Books Focusing on Sounds or Word Families

Abrons, M. *For Alice, A Palace.* Young Scott, 1966.

Barret, Judy. *Pickles Have Pimples and Other Silly Statements.* Athenum, 1986.

Barry, Katherine. *A Bug to Hug.* Young Scott, 1964.

Einsel, Walter. *Did You Ever See?* Scholastic, 1972.

Most, Bernard. *There's an Ant in Anthony.* Morrow, 1980.

Patz, Nancy. *Moses Supposes His Toeses Are Roses: And Seven Other Silly Old Rhymes.* Harcourt, 1983.

Raskin, Ellen. *"Who," Said Sue, "Said WHOO?"* Anthenum, 1973.

Shaw, Nancy. *Sheep in a Jeep.* Houghton Mifflin, 1986.

Thomas, Patricia. *"There are Rocks in my Socks," Said the Ox to the Fox*. Lothrop, 1979.

Figurative Language

Books Focusing on Rhyme and Rhythm (Predictable Books)

Carle, Eric. *The Very Busy Spider*. Philomel, 1984.

Galdone, Paul. *The Teeny Tiny Woman*. Clarion, 1984.

Hill, Eric. *Spot Goes to the Beach*. Putnam, 1985.

Martin, Bill Jr. *Brown Bear, Brown Bear, What Do You See?* Holt, Rinehart, & Winston, 1983.

Mayer. Mercer. *All By Myself*. Western Publishing Company, 1983.

Nerlove, Miriam. *I Meant to Clean My Room Today*. McElderry, 1988.

Numeroff, Laura. *If You Gave a Mouse a Cookie*. Harper & Row, 1985.

Sendak, Maurice. *Chicken Soup with Rice*. Scholastic, 1962.

Voirst, Judith. *Alexander and the Terrible, Horrible, No Good, Very Bad Day*. Atheneum, 1972.

Books Focusing on Word Play

Adler, David A. *The Carsick Zebra and Other Animal Riddles*. Holiday House, 1983.

Bishop, Ann. *Hello, Mr. Chips*. Dutton, 1982.

Cole, William, and Mike Thaler. *Monster Knock Knocks*. Archway Pocket Books, 1982.

Epsy, Willard R. *A Children's Almanac of Words at Play*. Crown, 1983.

Keller, Charles. *News Breaks*. Prentice Hall, 1980.

Stokes, Jack. *Monster Madness*. Doubleday, 1981.

Thaler, Mike. *Soup With Quackers*. Franklin Watts, 1976.

Tremain, Ruthven. *Fooling Around With Words*. Greenwillow, 1976.

Books Focusing on Language Play

Hall, Rich. *Sniglets*. Macmillan/Collier, 1984.

Keller, Charles. *Daffynitions*. Prentice Hall, 1976.

Kohl, Herbert L. *A Book of Puzzlements: Play and Invention With Language*. Schocken Books, 1981.

Books Focusing on Idioms

Abel, Alison M. *Make Hay While the Sun Shines*. London: Faber & Faber, 1977.

Cox, J.A. *Put Your Foot in Your Mouth*. Random, 1980.

Folsom, Marcia and Michael. *Easy as Pie: A Guessing Game of Sayings*. Clarion, 1985.

Krensky, Stephen. *Castles in the Air and Other Tales*. Atheneum, 1979.

Thayer, Jane. *Try Your Hand*. Morrown, 1979.

Books Focusing on Homonyms

Bossom, Naomi. *A Scale Full of Fish, and Other Turnabouts*. Greenwillow, 1979.

Clifford, Eth. *A Bear Before Breakfast*. Putnam, 1962.

Gwynne, Fred. *A Chocolate Moose for Dinner*. Dutton, 1973.

Gwynne, Fred. *The King Who Rained*. Windmill Press, 1970.

Parrish, Peggy. *Amelia Bedelia*. Harper, 1963.

Wiseman, Bernard. *Morris Goes to School*. Harper & Row, 1970.

Books Focusing on Antonyms

Burningham, John. *John Burningham's Opposites*. Crown, 1986.

Crother, Robert. *The Most Amazing Hide-and-Seek Opposites Book*. Viking, 1985.

Herfter, Richard. *Yes and No: A Book of Opposites*. Strawberry, 1975.

Hoban, Tana. *Push, Pull, Empty, Full: A Book of Opposites*. Macmillan, 1972.

Hulme, Susan. *Let's Look for Opposites*. Coward, 1984.

McMillan, Bruce. *Becca Backward, Becca Forward*. Lothrop, 1986.

Maestro, Betsy and Guilio. *Traffic: A Book of Opposites*. Crown, 1981.

Spier, Peter. *Fast-Slow, High-Low: A Book of Opposites*. Doubleday, 1972.

Wilbur, Richard. *Opposites*. Harcourt, 1973.

Books Focusing on Alliteration

Barrett, Judi. *A Snake Is Totally Tail*. Atheneum, 1983.

Bayley, Nicola. *One Old Oxford Ox*. Atheneum, 1977.

Carle, Eric. *All About Arthur, an Absolutely Absurd Ape*. Watts, 1974.

Hilgartner, Beth. *Great Gorilla Grins: An Abundance of Animal Alliterations*. Little, Brown, 1977.

Books Focusing on Onomatopoeia

Allen, Pamela. *Bertie and the Bear*. Coward, 1984.

Brown, Margaret Wise. *Shhhh--BANG!! A Whispering Book.* Harper, 1943.

Burningham, John. *Noisy Words Series: Slam Bang, Jangle Twank, Cluck Baa, Skip Trip, Sniff Shout, Wobble Pop.* Viking, 1986.

Lemieux, Michele. *What's That Noise?* Morrown, 1985.

Reid, Alistair. *Ounce, Dice Trice.* Gregg, 1980.

Richter, Mischa. *Quack?* Harper, 1978.

Spier, Peter. *Crash!! Bang!! Boom!!* Doubleday, 1972.

Spier, Peter. *Gobble, Growl, Grunt.* Doubleday, 1971.

Books Focusing on Similes

Asch, Frank. *I Can Blink.* Crown, 1986.

Asch, Frank. *I Can Roar.* Crown, 1986.

Krauss, Robert. *My Son the Mouse.* Windmill, 1977.

Lewin, Hugh. *Jafta.* Carolrhoda, 1983.

Ormerod, Jan. *Just Like Me.* Lothrop, 1986.

Parts of Speech

Books Focusing on Adjectives

Boynton, Sandra. *A Is For Angry.* Workman, 1983.

Carle, Eric. *The Very Hungry Caterpillar.* Philomel, 1987.

Chorao, Kay. *Kate's Quilt.* Dutton, 1982.

Heller, Ruth. *Many Luscious Lollipops: A Book About Adjectives.* Grosset and Dunlap, 1989.

Hoban, Tana. *A Children's Zoo*. Greenwillow, 1981.

Keats, Ezra. *Peter's Chair*. Harper & Row, 1967.

Maestro, Besty and Guilio. *On the Go: A Book of Adjectives*. Crown, 1979.

Viorst, Judith. *My Mama Says*. Atheneum, 1975.

Books Focusing on Singular and Plural Nouns

Barton, Byron. *Boats*. Crowell, 1986.

Ets, Marie Hall. *In the Forest*. Viking, 1944.

Peppe, Rodney. *Humphrey the Number Horse*. Viking, 1978.

Terban, Marvin. *Your Foot's on My Feet! And Other Tricky Nouns*. Clarion, 1986.

Books Focusing on Personal Pronouns

Brown, Marc. *Arthur's Nose*. Little, Brown, & Co.,1976.

Keller, Holly. *Geraldine's Blanket*. Greenwillow, 1984.

Mayer, Mercer. *Hiccup*. Dial Books for Young Readers, 1976.

Marshall, James. *George and Martha*. Houghton Mifflin, 1973.

McPhail, David. *Emma's Pet*. Dutton, 1985.

Roffrey, Maureen. *Look, There's My Hat*. Putnam, 1984.

Books Focusing on Verbs

Barton, Byron. *Building a House*. Greenwillow, 1981.

Brown, Margaret Wise. *Goodnight Moon*. Harper & Row, 1947.

Ets, Marie Hall. *In The Forest.* Viking, 1944.

Hutchins, Pat. *Good-Night Owl!* Macmillan, 1972.

Isadora, Rachel. *Ben's Trumpet.* Greenwillow, 1979.

McMillan, Bruce. *Kitten Can...A Concept Book.* Lothrop, 1984.

Maestro, Betsy and Guilio. *Busy Day. A Book of Action Words.* Crown, 1978.

Pinkwater, Daniel Manus. *The Big Orange Splot.* Scholastic, 1977.

Terban, Marvin. *I Think I Thought and Other Tricky Verbs.* Clarion, 1984.

Books Focusing on Prepositions

Banchek, Linda. *Snake In, Snake Out.* Crowell, 1978.

Bernstain, Stan. *Inside, Outside, Upside Down.* Random House, 1968.

Brown, Ruth. *A Dark, Dark Tale.* Dial Books for Young Readers, 1981.

Dunrae, Olivier. *Mogwogs on the March!* Holiday House, 1985.

Hoban, Tana. *Over, Under, Through, and Other Spatial Concepts.* Macmillan, 1973.

Hutchins, Pat. *Rosie's Walk.* Macmillan, 1968.

Gackenbach, Dick. *Harry and the Terrible Whatzit.* Clarion, 1984.

Ormerod, Jan. *Reading.* Lothrop, 1985.

Reading Comprehension

Books That Focus on Sequencing

Carle, Eric. *The Very Hungry Caterpillar.* World, 1960.

Christian, Mary. *Nothing Much Happened Today*. Addison Wesley, 1973.

Domanska, Janina. *Busy Monday Morning*. Greenwillow, 1985.

Gilham, Bill. *What Happened Next?* Putnam, 1985.

Maestro, Betsy and Guilio. *Through The Year With Harriet*. Crown, 1985.

Tafuri, Nancy. *All Year Long*. Greenwillow, 1983.

Books That Focus on Following Directions

Brown, Marc. *Hand Rhymes*. Dutton, 1985.

Martin, Liz. *Viking Little Chef Series: Making Pizza, Making Muffins, Making Pretzels, Making Chocolate Chip Cookies*. Viking, 1986.

Parish, Peggy. *Beginning Mobiles*. Macmillan, 1979.

Rockwell, Harlow. *I Did It*. Macmillan, 1974.

Williams, Vera. *Three Days on a River in a Red Canoe*. Greenwillow, 1980.

Books That Focus on Drawing Conclusions

Arden Ailliam. *The Three Investigators in the Mystery of the Wrecker's Rock*. Random, 1986.

Bester, Roger. *Guess What?* Crown, 1980.

Ecke, Wolfgang. *The Face at the Window*. Prentice, 1980.

Emberley, Ed. *Ed Emberley's Amazing Look Through Book*. Little, Brown, 1979.

Sobol, Donald J. *Encyclopedia Brown Sets The Pace*. Four Winds Press, 1982.

Vivelo, Jackie. *Super Sleuth. Twelve Solve-It-Yourself Mysteries.* Putnam, 1985.

Books That Focus on Creative Thinking

Brandenburg, Fanz. *What Can You Make Of It?* Greenwillow, 1977.

Crews, Donald. *Ten Black Dots.* Greenwillow, 1986.

Gardner, Beau. *The Turn About, Think About, Look About Book.* Lothrop, 1980.

Gillham, Bill. *What Can You Do?* Putnam, 1986.

Moffett, Marta. *A Flower Pot Is Not a Hat.* Dutton, 1972.

Radlaur, Ruth. *What Can You Do with a Box?* Children's Press, 1973.

Mathematics

Books That Focus on Counting/Numbers

Anno, Mitsumsas. *Counting House.* Philomel Books, 1982.

Blumenthal, Nancy. *Count-A-Saurus.* Macmillan, 1987.

Brown, Marc. *One, Two, Three.* Little Brown, 1976.

Dee, Ruby. *Two Ways to Count to 10.* Henry Holt, 1988.

Miller, Jane. *Farm Counting Book.* Prentice Hall, 1983.

Books That Focus on Money Concepts

Schwartz, David. *If You Made a Million.* Lathrop, 1989.

Williams, Vera B. *A Chair for My Mother.* Prentice Hall, 1967.

Books That Focus on Time

Baum, Arline & Joseph. *One Bright Monday Morning*. Random House, 1962.

dePaola, Tomie. *Charlie Needs a Clock*. Prentice Hall, 1973.

Sendak, Maurice. *Chicken Soup with Rice*. Scholastic, 1962.

Books That Focus on Measurement

Allen, Pamela. *Who Sank the Boat?* Rigby Education,1982.

Parkes, Brenda and Judith Smith. *The Enormous Watermelon*. Rigby Education, 1986.

Books That Focus on Shapes

Adler, David. *Three-D, Two-D*. Crowell, 1975.

Atwood, Ann. *The Little Circle*. Scribner, 1967.

Brown, Marcia Joan. *Listen to a Shape*. Watts, 1979.

Budney, Blossom. *A Kiss Is Round*. Lothrop, 1954.

Friskey, Margaret. *Three Sides and the Round One*. Children's Press, 1973.

Hoban, Tana. *Circles, Triangles, and Squares*. Macmillan, 1970.

Silverstein, Shell. *The Missing Piece*. Harper and Row, 1976.

Themes

Looking Different

Anderson, Hans Christian. *The Ugly Duckling*. Macmillan, 1955.

Blume, Judy S. *Freckle Juice*. Four Winds, 1971.

Getting Along/Friendship

Cleary, Beverly. *Ramona the Pest*. Morrown, 1968.

Concord, Ellen. *Anything For a Friend*. Little, Brown, 1979.

Morrow, Emily. *Just My Luck*. Unicorn, 1982.

Smith, Doris B. *Laura Upside-Down*. Viking, 1984.

Self-Confidence

Beim, Jerrold. *The Smallest Boy in the Class*. Morrow, 1949.

Greene, Bette. *Get On Out Of Here, Philip Hall*. Dial Books, 1981.

Holcomb, Nan. *Patrick and Emma Lou*. Turtle Books, 1989.

Manes, Stephen. *Be a Perfect Person in Just Three Days*. Clarion, 1982.

Death

Hermes, Patricia. *You Shouldn't Have to Say Goodbye*. Harcourt Brace Jovanovich, 1982.

Paterson, Katherine. *Bridge to Terabithia*. Thomas Crowell, 1977.

Fears

Bachmann, Evelyn T. *Tressa*. Viking, 1966.

Dalgliesh, Alice. *The Courage of Sarah Noble*. Scribner's, 1954.

Weiman, Eiveen. *Which Way Courage?* Atheneum, 1981.

Prejudice/Discrimination

Blue, Rose. *The Preacher's Kid*. Watts, 1975.

Miner, Jane C. *Navajo Victory: Being a Native American*. Crestwood, 1982.

Miner, Jane C. *The Tough Guy: Black in a White World*. Crestwood, 1982.

Taves, Isabella. *Not Bad for a Girl*. Evans, 1972.

Disabilities

Aiello, Barbara and Jeffrey Shulman. *It's Your Turn at Bat*. Twenty-First Century Books, 1988.

Becker, Shirley. *Buddy's Shadow*. Turtle Books, 1992.

Byars, Betsy. *Summer of the Swans*. Viking, 1974.

Emmert, Michelle. *I'm the Big Sister Now*. Albert Whitman & Co., 1989.

Fassler, Joan. *Howie Helps Himself*. Whitman & Co., 1975.

Gould, Marilyn. *Golden Daffodils*. Addison-Wesley, 1982.

Holcomb, Nan. *Sarah's Surprise*. Turtle Books, 1990.

Kneeland, Linda. *Cookie*. Turtle Books, 1989.

Litchfield, Ada. *A Button in Her Ear*. Whitman, 1976.

Mathis, Sharon. *Ray Charles*. Thomas Y. Crowell, 1973.

Mayer, Gina and Mercer. *A Very Special Critter*. Western Publishing Company, 1992.

References

Athney, I. (1971). Synthesis of papers on language development and reading. *Reading Research Quarterly*, 7 (1), 11-15.

Cushing-McWilliams, P. University of North Carolina, Chapel Hill, N.C.

Durkin, D. (1970). *Teaching Them to Read*. Boston: Allyn & Bacon.

Gebers, Jane L. (1990). *Books Are for Talking, Too!* Arizona: Communication Skill Builders

Goodall, G. (1964). In Shelly Umans, *Designs for Reading Programs*. New York: Teachers College Press.

Goossens', C. & Crain, S. (1986). *Augmentative Communication: Intervention Resource*. Birmingham, AL: University of Alabama at Birmingham.

Kaiser, P. (1990). Writing for nonreaders: storytelling with miniatures. *Writing Teacher*, 111 (5), 14-17.

Koppenhaver, D.A., Coleman, P.P., Kalman, S.L., & Yoder, D.E. (1991). The implications of emergent literacy research for children with developmental disabilities. *American Journal of Speech Language Pathology*, 1 (1), 38-44.

Koppenhaver, D.A., Evans, D.A., & Yoder, D.E. (1991). Childhood reading and writing experiences of literate adults with severe speech and physical impairments. *Augmentative and Alternative Communication*, 7 (1), 20-33.

Koppenhaver, D.A., & Yoder, D.E. (1988). Independent reading practice. *Aug-Communique: N.C. Augmentative Communication Newsletter*, 6 (3), 9-11.

Koppenhaver, D.A. & Yoder, D.E. (1992). Literacy issues in persons with severe speech and physical impairments. In R. Gaylord-Ross (Eds.), *Research and Issues in Special Education* (pp.156-201). New York: Columbia University, Teachers College Press.

Koppenhaver, D.A. & Yoder, D.E. (1992). Literacy learning of children with severe speech and physical impairments in school settings. *Seminars in Speech and Language*, 13 (2), 143-153.

May, F. (1986). *Reading As Communication: An Interactive Approach*. Columbus, OH: Merrill Publishing Co.

McDonald, E.T. & Shultz, A. (1973). Communication boards for cerebral palsied children. *Journal of Speech and Hearing Disorders*. 38, 73-88.

McGee, L.M., & Richgels, D.J. (1990). *Literacy's Beginnings: Supporting Young Readers and Writers*. Boston, MA: Allyn & Bacon, Inc.

McNairn, P. (1992, June). *Literacy for Nonverbal Children*. Paper presented at the annual National Educational Computing Conference, Dallas, Texas.

McNairn, P., & Shioleno, C. (1992, June). Literacy skills for nonverbal children. *Augmentative and Alternative Communication*, 8 (2), 153.

McNairn, P., & Shioleno, C. (1992, April). *Using The Language of the Learner: Literacy Skills for Nonverbal Children*. Paper presented at the annual Texas Speech & Hearing Association, San Antonio, Texas.

McNairn, P., & Shioleno, C. (1992) *Quick Tech Activities for Literacy*. Illinois: Don Johnston Developmental Equipment, Inc.

Merritt, J.E. (ed.). (1974). *New Horizons in Reading: Proceedings of the Fifth IRA World Congress on Reading*. Delaware: International Reading Association.

Meyers, L. (1984). Unique contributions of microcomputers to language intervention with handicapped children. *Seminars in Speech and Language*, 5 (1), 23-33.

Meyers, L. (1987, Feb./Mar.). Bypassing the prerequisites: the computer as a language scaffold. *Closing the Gap*, 19-20.

Nippold, M., Schartz, I., & Lewis, M. (1992). Analyzing the potential benefit of microcomputer use for teaching figurative language.

American Journal of Speech-Language Pathology: A Journal of Clinical Practice, 1 (2), 36-43.

Page, J., and Stewart, S. (1985). Story grammar skills in school-aged children. *Topics in Language Disorders* 5, 16-29.

Rothlein, Liz, & Meinbach, Anita M. (1991). *The Literature Connection*. Glenview, Illinois: Scott, Foresman and Company.

Trelease, J. (1985). *The Read Aloud Handbook*. New York: Penguin Books.

Wang, M. (1992). *Adaptive Education Strategies*. Baltimore, MD: Paul Brookes Publishing Co.

Wilkinson, A. (1971). *The Foundations of Language, Talking, and Reading in Young Children*. London: Oxford University Press.

About the Authors

Peggi McNairn, Ph.D., CCC/SLP, is a licensed Speech/Language Pathologist who received her Master of Science degree in Communication Pathology and her Ph.D. in Education. Her clinical experience in public schools, hospitals, clinics, rehabilitation centers, and nursing homes has focused upon the evaluation and implementation of augmentative communication and adapted technology for the physically and mentally challenged. She currently serves on the Executive Board for the Texas Society for Augmentative and Alternative Communication and is an active member of the Texas Speech and Hearing Association's Augmentative Communication Task Force.

Cindy Shioleno, M.Ed., received her Master of Education in Early Childhood and has a wide variety of experiences as an educator, administrator, supervisor, and curriculum writer in both general and special education. She is currently an educational specialist for the state of Texas where she provides technical assistance and training in the area of assistive technology.

In addition to presentations at the state, national, and international level, the authors have published numerous articles on a variety of topics including adapted computer access, interdisciplinary team training, and literacy development in nonverbal children. They co-authored the book *Quick Tech Activities for Literacy* and are currently working on a manuscript for literacy-based music therapy for individuals with special needs.

Quick Tech Activities for Literacy

This book is authored by Peggi McNairn, Ph.D., CCC/SLP and Cindy Shioleno, M.Ed. and published by Don Johnston Developmental Equipment, Inc. It outlines fast, effective, and simple strategies for modifying the language arts curriculum for physically and mentally challenged students. The activities provided help to develop and enhance literacy skills through meaningful, interactive learning using light-tech devices. Step-by-step directions and illustrations are provided.

What's in Quick Tech Activities for Literacy?

Part One: Quick Tech Tools - describes five ligh-tech devices that the activities are designed around. This section gives a brief description of each device and includes directions for making the devices if appropriate.

Part Two: 21 Quick Tech Literacy Activities. Each activity includes:
- Literacy Skill
- Student Goal
- Materials
- Rationale
- Directions
- Ideas
- Linking Activities
- Poems, Pictures, Word Cards, and/or Duplication Masters

Part Three: Final Notes and Tips - Contains a miscellaneous collection of ideas and resources for expanding literacy activities.

Quick Tech I.D.E.A.S.S.
215 Spanish Moss
Arlington, Texas 76018
(817) 468-0927

QTY	ITEM	No.	UNIT PRICE	TOTAL COST
	Quick Tech Activities for Literacy	LT104	$25.00	
			Sub-Total	
			Shipping & Handling - 10%	
			Tax (7.8% TX only)	
			TOTAL AMOUNT	

Quick Tech I.D.E.A.S.S.

215 Spanish Moss
Arlington, TX 76018
(817) 468-0927

The ReadIt Vest™

Similar in design to a communication vest, the ReadItVest is constructed of lightweight, Velcro®-sensitive fabric. Provides an excellent background for literacy development activities.
LT101 $15.00

The ReadIt Window™

An eye-gaze communication display made of clear, light-weight lexan. The 18" x 18" window can be attached to a computer monitor or the ReadIt Frame for literacy activities.
LT 102 $20.00

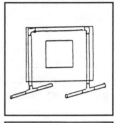

The ReadIt Frame™

A 20" x 24" frame constructed from durable CPVC pipe; the ReadIt Frame can be attached to a wheelchair tray or placed on a table top.
LT 103 $15.00

Miniature Objects - $5.00 a set
Old Lady and the Fly - MO 101
I Want a Pet - MO 102
At the Zoo - MO 103

Ship to:

Name _____

Address _____

City _____ State _____ Zip _____

QTY	ITEM	No.	Unit Price	Total Price
			Subtotal	
		Shipping & Handling - 10%		
		Tax (7.8% TX only)		
		TOTAL AMOUNT		

Units
Units is a 208 page book consisting of 9 units for preschool and elementary classrooms. Individual unit titles are Shapes, My Body, Indian, Winter Fun, Alphabet, Animals, Community Workers, Earth, and Transportation. Each unit has lessons in art, music, cooking, and literacy. Communication overlays, in two sizes, are also provided in two configurations (9 and 36 cell). The displays may be used separately or on the Wolf. A Wolf Cap will also be available for the book.

Total Augmentative Communication In The Early Childhood Classroom
A 248 page comprehensive guide to augmentative communication and technology. The book is full of practical ideas and information. Topics covered include manual communication boards, sign language, facilitated communication, powered mobility, voice-output, picture and symbol systems, emergent literacy skills, emergent math, objectives and evaluation of performance, teaching techniques, instructional materials strategies, and an extensive list of resources. This is an exceptional book including many illustrations and examples.

The Preschool AAC Checklist (3 Copies) And Video
The checklists are 116 page booklets for teacher guidance and for tracking students progress in augmentative communication. The booklets also contain symbols and student remediation materials. A 20 minute video provides a good introduction.

What's In Your Home?
What's In Your Community?
Low-level workbooks that each student may keep as their own. The books are designed for students who need practice with everyday vocabulary, such as "chair", "store", and "bedroom". Each workbook includes discussion sheets, study sheets, vocabulary worksheets, unit reviews, and unit review worksheets.

Life Experiences Kit
A unique set of eleven different "lesson plans" designed for non-speech or limited speech students. The plans and materials teach specific daily life activity skills, such as "Make Juice", "Wash Hands", and "Go Restaurant". Included are symbol instructions sheets and communication boards.

Picture Symbol Lotto
This special lotto game is set up in color coded sections of verbs, adjectives and nouns. An excellent opportunity to reinforce common vocabulary and color-coding cues used on communication boards.

Holiday Kit
The Holiday Kit is a set of low level materials based on holidays designed to stimulate enthusiasm, interest, and conversation in your clients. The kit includes a folder and 9 pre-made communication boards in both 1" and 2" sizes. Symbol masters for an additional 15 holidays are also included.

Zoo Kit
The Zoo Kit expands symbol reading and sentence building skills so that the symbol users may create their own story. It includes worksheets, stamps, and lesson plans with the zoo and animals as the topic.

For further information on these products and others, please call or write for our free brochure.

Mayer-Johnson Co.
P.O. Box 1579
Solana Beach, CA 92075-1579
U.S.A.
(619) 550-0084
(619) 550-0449 FAX